WOMEN PAINTERS IN ROME

Guidebook

edited by
Ilaria Arcangeli

OFFICINA LIBRARIA

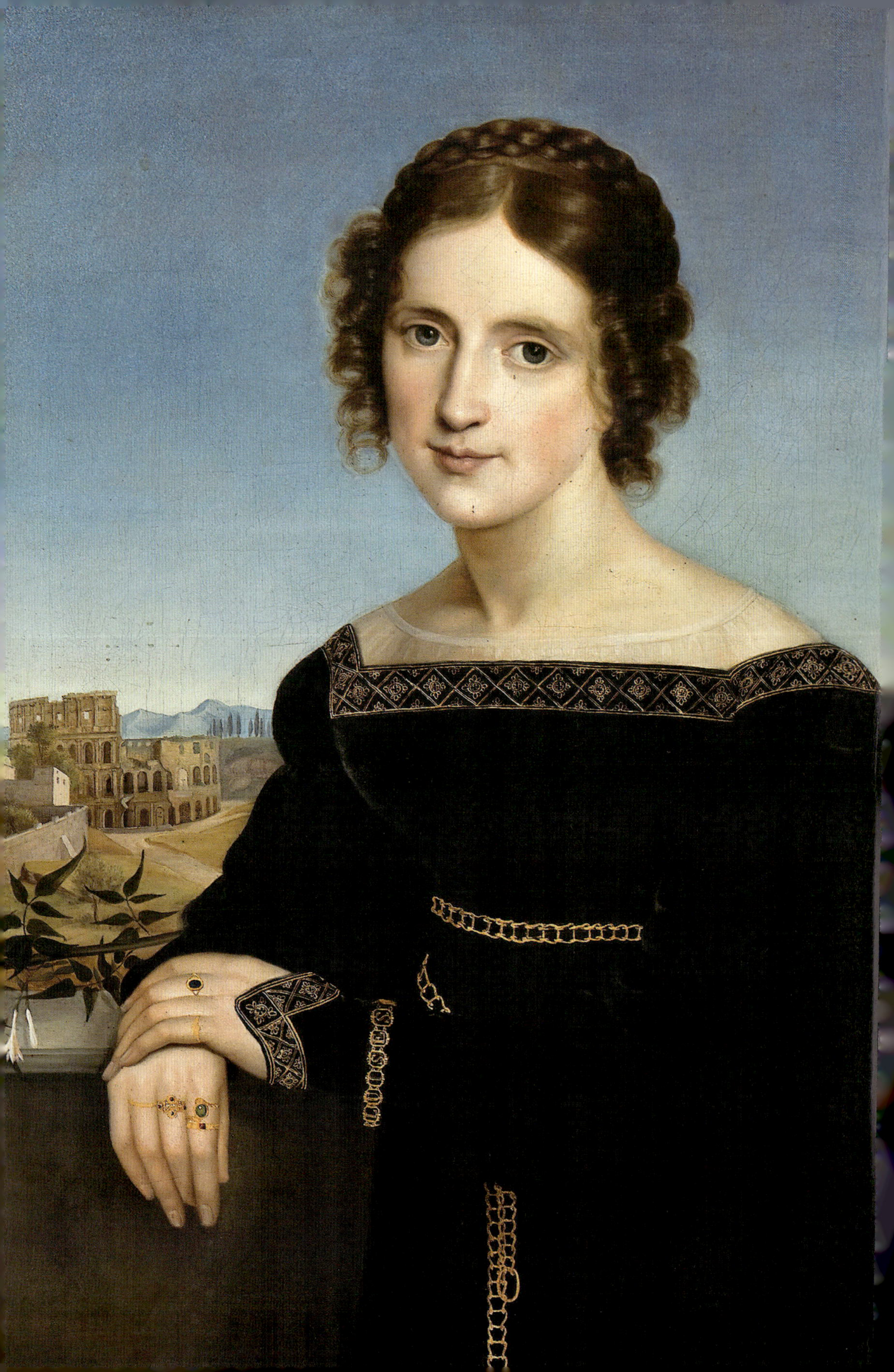

PREFACE

The exhibition *Roma pittrice. Artiste al lavoro tra XVI e XIX secolo* / Rome paints. Women Artists at Work Between the 16th and 19th Centuries (Palazzo Braschi–Museo di Roma, 25 October 2024 – 23 March 2025) aims to give due prominence to the women artists who worked in Rome during the modern period. Rome is considered as a cultural epicentre and symbol of the establishment of women in the arts at a time dominated by men, simultaneously acting as a metaphor for the many women who contributed to its prestige.

The studies undertaken in preparation for the exhibition were focused on 56 women artists who worked permanently or temporarily in Rome. This reconstruction started from the Capitoline collections before moving on to other Italian and international institutions. In recent decades, research on women's art has intensified in an effort to fill the historiographical gaps that have often relegated women to minor roles. Women artists, overlooked in the documents or whose works were mistaken for those of male masters, have been rediscovered through sporadic mentions in diaries, signatures, correspondences and self-portraits. This has made it possible at least in part to write the history of women's art.

Women artists such as Lavinia Fontana and Artemisia Gentileschi have emerged as prominent figures, universally recognized for their contribution to art. Lavinia, originally from Bologna, brought with her a new model of the cultured woman, whilst Artemisia attempted to establish herself in an environment still ruled by prejudices and legal limitations for women. The opportunities available to women artists in Rome were often linked to family circumstances and access to the academies, like that of San Luca, essential for gaining visibility.

Despite the difficulties of the context in which they worked, women artists in Rome contributed to the development of the arts, sharing studios and interests with their male colleagues in a cosmopolitan city that drew Italian and foreign talents. Though Rome was not home in the 19th century to great international exhibitions like those held in France or England, it remained a vital centre for artistic production.

This guide aims to introduce the studies conducted in preparation for the exhibition to a much wider audience. The introductory essay by Ilaria Arcangeli thus surveys the main stages in the long and complex road to the establishment of women artists in Rome. It is followed by the biographies reconstructed by the various scholars who have collaborated on the exhibition catalogue.

The work is completed by an exhaustive map of Rome accompanied by a commentary that guides visitors around the city to discover the many works by women artists preserved in accessible places.

Ilaria Miarelli Mariani and *Raffaella Morselli*

Luise Seidler, *Portrait of Franziska ("Fanny") Caspers*, 1818–19. Copenaghen, Thorvaldsens Museum.

THE WOMEN OF THE ETERNAL CITY

Ilaria Arcangeli

The *Eternal City* is a definition coined by the Latin poets that for centuries has influenced the world's perception of Rome. The entire city with its squares, monuments and churches is a symbol of continuity between past and present: Rome's history and culture have forged and defined the identity of the West. As the centre of the Christian world, it has for centuries been a hub for exchanges and the emergence of new artistic phenomena that have influenced the form of the city. Women have left their own imprint on the evolution of this image, visible or more inconspicuous, funding the construction of palaces, churches and monasteries, and helping to consolidate the political power of noble Roman and foreign families.

Due in part to the significant presence of the Papal States, women were a minority in the city's population, accounting for under 38% in 1600 and, despite a gradual increase, for only 48.5% in 1869. As part of Roman society, they contributed to the growth of the city with their labour. Women worked in a wide range of occupations: as servants and maids, seamstresses and embroiderers, sellers of vegetables and other foods, laundresses, bakers, spinners and weavers, but also as the keepers of inns and lodging houses, schoolteachers, nurses and midwives, sex workers, artists and craftswomen employed in the city's construction sites.

From 1506, men and women worked together to build and decorate the world's most important church, St Peter's Basilica, dividing up duties and tasks. A professional system took shape made up of skilled and specialized women artists, educated women and manual labourers, alongside craftswomen chosen for their artistic skills and not just as the heirs or wives of deceased male workers. In this context, a very interesting instance that remains to be reconstructed is that of Isabella d'Arcangelo, who was involved in the decorative worksite for the rooms in the Vatican Apostolic Library under the direction of Cesare Nebbia. Her name appears in an inscription in the scene depicting the Council of Trent, where she is said to originate from Jesi, a small town in the Marche region. Together with her last name, this suggests that she may have been related to the painter Arcangelo Aquilini (1560–1611). She was the only woman artist engaged on the worksite to have actually signed her work and must have been well aware of the exceptional nature of her role in the 1570s.

In contrast to other Italian cities, where women artists had been present since the 15th century, particularly in the monastic sphere (examples include Caterina Vigri in Bologna and Sister Eufrasia Burlamacchi in Lucca), the first documented women artists only appeared in Rome in the second half of the 16th century.

* Further details on the issues discussed in this essay can be found in the Italian language catalogue of the exhibition *Roma pittrice. Artiste al lavoro tra XVI e XIX secolo*, exhib. cat. (Rome 2024–25), ed. by Ilaria Miarelli Mariani and Raffaella Morselli with Ilaria Arcangeli. Rome: Officina Libraria, 2024.

Arrivals and Departures from Rome: Lavinia Fontana and Artemisia Gentileschi

The city of the popes differed in many ways from the flourishing Bologna, which by the end of the 16th century could already boast numerous well-established women artists and as many in training. Undoubtedly, the first woman artist in demand from Roman patrons was Lavinia Fontana, who had trained in Bologna and arrived in the city around 1604, as the guest first of Cardinal Alessandro d'Este and then of Domenico Attavanti. Already highly respected for her talent, she was officially invited to Rome in 1600 thanks to the success of *The Vision of St Hyacinth*, sent for the church of Santa Sabina where it can still be admired today. Her most important works of this period include the lost altarpiece with the *Stoning of St Stephen* for the Roman Basilica of San Paolo Fuori le Mura, a highly prestigious commission that helped to consolidate her reputation in the capital. Lavinia worked in an environment dominated by male painters, but her talent allowed her to compete on an equal footing with male colleagues. She even obtained equal pay, though her husband, Giovan Paolo Zappi, always took charge of her contracts and negotiations. Despite some criticisms, including from the painter Giovanni Baglione, who found it difficult to tolerate a woman succeeding in a male-dominated field, Lavinia was respected for the quality of her works. She also received praise for her portraits, including that of Pope Paul V, her great admirer. In the painting now in the Museo di Capodimonte in Naples, *Christ and the Samaritan Woman*, with a stretch of the Aurelian Walls incorporated into the background, the painter demonstrates the personal growth that she experienced in contact with the inspirations of contemporary Roman painting, starting from the treatment of light used to create new three-dimensional effects. Though she partially withdrew from the public eye to become a Capuchin laywoman in the final years of her life, Lavinia continued to work on important projects such as the Rivaldi chapel in the church of Santa Maria della Pace. Her refined technique is clearly apparent in the representations of the women saints depicted here and in the portraits of her patrons, confirmation of her extraordinary talent. She died in Rome in 1614, leaving a legacy of works admired for their elegance and innovation.

At around the same time, the Roman Artemisia Gentileschi, daughter of the painter Orazio Lomi Gentileschi, was training in the city. After leaving in 1612 she returned a few years later, now very famous, before departing for good in 1626. She lived at her home-workshop in Via Paolina and then in Via della Croce, growing up in a stimulating environment and dedicating herself to painting from a very early age. She studied using repertoires of engravings and through careful observation of the works of artists active in the city. The works of Caravaggio had a great influence on the young painter, as shown by the two different versions of *Judith and Holofernes* (Naples, Museo di Capodimonte; Florence, Gallerie degli Uffizi). Artemisia was in contact with numerous colleagues, like Simon Vouet who painted her portrait (Bergamo, Zaccaria Collection), and almost certainly befriended the painter Virginia da Vezzo, who married the French artist. She had ties to numerous other women active in the art world: Maddalena Corvini portrayed her as St Catherine of Alexandria (Fisher Collection); with Giovanna Garzoni she may have travelled to the English court in the late 1630s; she was certainly close to Costanza Connodoli, a candle painter for the Compagnia della Pietà della Nazione Fiorentina, as both were subjected to slanderous accusations for their ties to the painter Agostino Tassi.

Early Achievements: Rome's Academies Open Their Doors to Women

Admission to specialist associations and institutions remained off limits to women at least until 1580, when it was decided to allow the first four entry to the Compagnia di San Giuseppe di Terrasanta. Membership of this association, later known as the Accademia dei Virtuosi, was reserved for painters, sculptors and architects, and over the centuries many women connected to the art world belonged to it. The change was officially recognized with the bull of Pope Gregory XIII (1584). The four women admitted included Diana Scultori, the wife of Francesco Capirani, who, as a supporter of the Reformation, moved to Rome from Mantua in around 1573 to continue her career as a printmaker.

The same rule was only introduced at the Accademia di San Luca, founded in 1593, a few decades later. The 1607 statutes established that women artists could be admitted if they had attained a degree of fame and made a gift of one of their works to the institution. The explicit reference to the role of women was reiterated in the statutes of 1617, which clarified that they were not permitted to attend lectures and assemblies though they enjoyed all other "academic privileges". Gender-based exclusions seem to have remained in force until the 1790s.

The presence of numerous portraits and self-portraits in the collections of the Accademia di San Luca is clear evidence of the prestige attained by women artists. The 1633 inventory lists portraits of Sofonisba Anguissola (1532–1625) and Girolama Parasole. Some were commissioned subsequently to celebrate their subjects while others were gifts from the artists themselves. Often there are no official traces of their admission to the Academy and the lack of evidence that they ever lived in Rome suggests that many of these portraits were purely commemorative.

The oldest document confirming the presence of women in the academy is a list dated 1633 that includes both men and women as members of the institution. Among those mentioned are Caterina Ginnasi, Giovanna Garzoni and Giustiniana Guidotti. The latter died only a year after her appointment, so the document should be considered valid while her presence in subsequent lists should be interpreted as a tribute. Garzoni was admitted though she was not living in Rome, as she spent that year in Turin: we must assume that as this was an honorary position it did not require a constant presence. The same three artists are mentioned again in the 1651 list, alongside Anna Maria Vaiani and Felice Orlandi. Their names are accompanied by those of Lucia Neri and Ippolita de Biagi in the list drawn up between the late 17th and the early 18th century.

Engravers and Miniaturists: Towards Professionalisation

The fame achieved by Diana Scultori during her lifetime was undoubtedly a consequence of her move from Mantua to Rome. Here she was not just among the first women to be admitted to the future Accademia dei Virtuosi but was also granted a papal privilege to market prints from her copper plates, effectively supporting her family financially. Her talents as an engraver were already celebrated by her contemporaries and a coin was even struck in her honour. Scultori's artistic career, always supported by her husband Francesco Capirani, followed a similar path to that of her brother Adamo.

The presence of a supportive family who encouraged their inclination towards engraving seems to be a crucial factor in the success of these women and their strides towards professionalization. Girolama Cagnucci, known by the last name of her husband Rosato Parasole, was a skilled woodcutter and, though difficult to document, her contribution to the family workshop was probably on a par with that of her spouse. Indeed, during the last decades of the century the Cagnucci obtained numerous commissions to create series of illustrations for printed texts and Girolama herself left her initials on a plate representing a scene of martyrdom. We know little about her sister-in-law, Elisabetta Cattaneo, originally from Bergamo and a skilled embroiderer who perfected, or perhaps even learned, this ancient art, the most commonly practiced by women, at the school of Santa Caterina. The question remains whether she also practiced woodcut printing, since the embroidery patterns she published in Rome between 1595 and 1600 provide no more detailed information.

The Roman publishing sector was booming towards the end of the 16th century and the production of sacred images drawn from paintings by renowned artists and used to illustrate printed repertoires in various fields of knowledge commissioned by leading figures at the papal court increased demand, favouring the inclusion of some women in this lively cultural sphere. Prime among them was Teresa del Po, who began her career in this field before specializing in miniature painting after her move to Naples. Not unusually, Del Po collaborated with an artist, the unknown Angelica Roncalli, who made drawings that she then translated into print. Indications of collaboration and mutual support are very common, although it is not always possible to trace the trajectories of these

Lavinia Fontana, *First Self-Portrait at the Spinet*, 1575. Rome, Private Collection (detail).

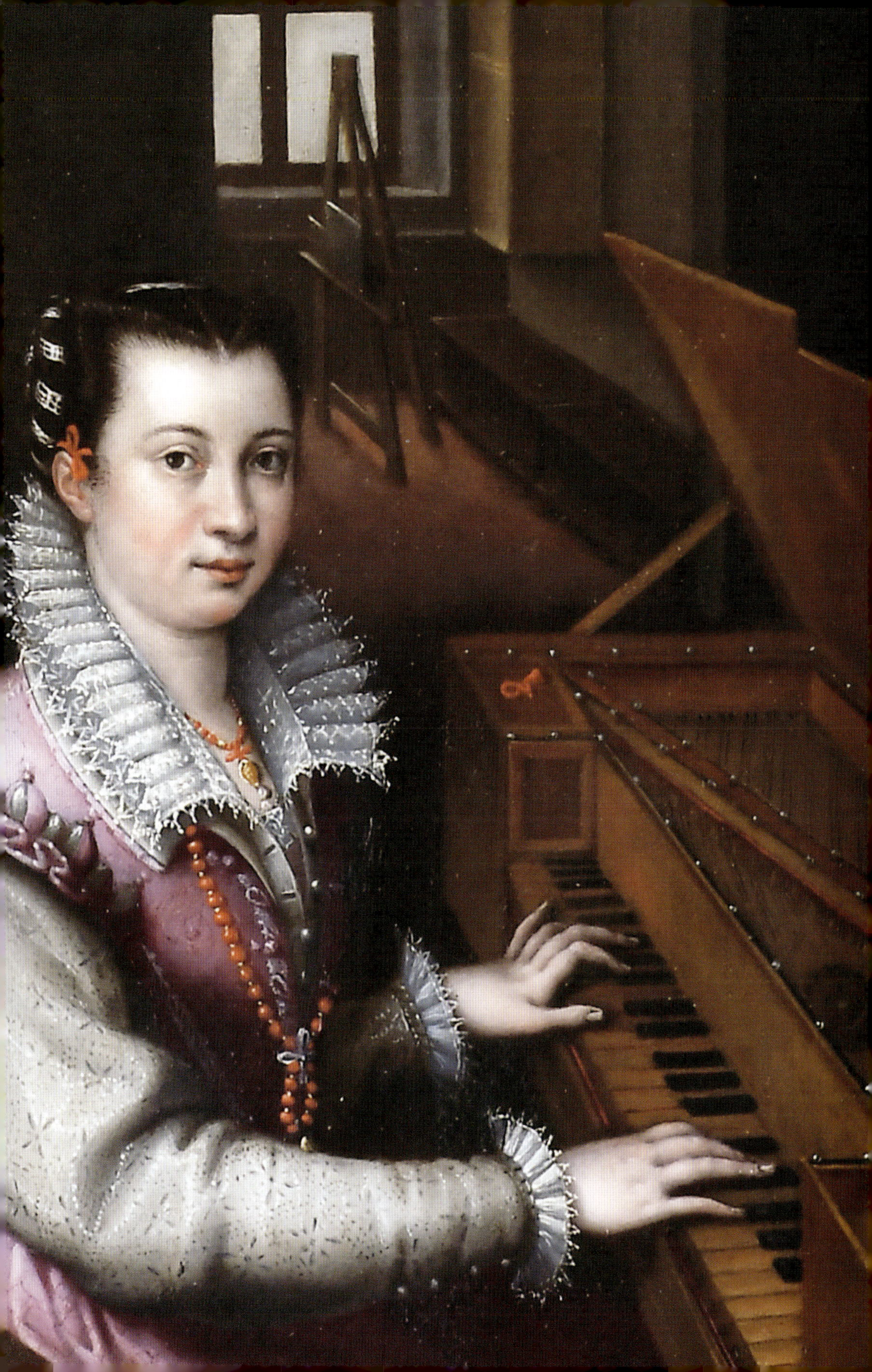

friendships. Certainly Maddalena Corvini, Giovanna Garzoni and Anna Maria Vaiani were in contact with one another, having participated in the decoration projects sponsored by Cassiano del Pozzo and the circles of the Barberini family. Such cooperative relationships facilitated the work of these women artists. Giovanna Garzoni became the Roman woman artist *par excellence*, even building a house near the artists' church of Santi Luca e Martina. Corvini was a highly celebrated miniaturist, though very few of her works are known, and also had a student, Anna Angelica Allegrini, daughter of the Orvietan painter Francesco. Anna Maria Vaiani arrived in Rome in her twenties and thanks to invaluable friendships like those with Galileo Galilei and Michelangelo Buonarroti the Younger came to work for the Barberini and in the Vatican, where she also executed some paintings.

Two Protagonists of Still Life Painting: Laura Bernasconi and Anna Stanchi

The 17th century saw the establishment of a sort of hierarchy of pictorial genres. Prince Vincenzo Giustiniani drew up a ranking composed of twelve genres in which still lives and landscapes appeared in fourth and seventh place respectively. Reviewing the inventories of the principal Roman and provincial princely collections suggests the predominance of such subjects, usually in a small format, which formed an essential element of home decor. These market demands explain why many painters in Rome specialized and devoted themselves to executing paintings with flowers and fruits, including serially, forming pendants or garlands surrounding a different subject. Decorations of this type were later extended to the walls and the mirrors of aristocratic palaces.

Two contemporary women artists whose work has re-emerged from the archive papers and from the signatures left on their works also specialized in this genre. Both worked closely with male colleagues: Laura Bernasconi trained with Mario Nuzzi, called Mario dei Fiori, specifically because of his specialization, while Anna Stanchi was the second oldest member of the Stanchi family who ran one of the most prolific still life workshops. Some information on Bernasconi is provided by her contemporaries, such as Filippo Titi and Lione Pascoli, who recognized her great talent in the execution of still lives. By contrast, Anna Stanchi has emerged from obscurity only thanks to the appearance on the art market of two signed paintings (2007, 2010). Following new research, we can now say that Stanchi lived for a long time with her older brother Giovanni, always considered the head of the workshop and credited with many paintings on the basis of stylistic comparisons or inventories, in which the Stanchi name often appears. It should also be borne in mind that the family expanded when Anna married Claudio Pionier, a French artist on whom no further information is available. For many years, they had a home-workshop in Via Paolina, adjacent to that of the famous French painter Nicolas Poussin. The high quality of the paintings signed by Anna and her age, only a few years younger than Giovanni, suggests that many of the works attributed to the elder brother alone might in fact reflect a close collaboration between the two.

For Laura Bernasconi, no sources have yet been found that clarify her origins and entry into the workshop of Rome's most sought-after still life painter. Her skills allowed her to sell her paintings in the workshop of Pellegrino Peri, one of the most successful art dealers of the time.

To date, we do not know other names of women painters who dedicated themselves to this genre of art, though there were certainly others. Partial confirmation of this comes from a note in the inventory of the collector Sisino Poli of 1697, which records two paintings of flowers by an unidentified woman.

Art and Culture in the Enclosed Space of Convents

Another category of women artists comprises those working in convents on altarpieces or minor decorations to embellish the interiors, far removed from market dynamics and often on direct assignment from the prioress. One such artist was Lucrina Fetti, who left Rome in 1614 with her brother Domenico and moved to Mantua where she entered the convent of Sant'Orsola, founded by Margherita Gonzaga, her main patron. In her paintings, Sister Lucrina always proudly signed herself "from Rome".

Unfortunately, few sources are available on artists working in Roman convents. One of the oldest indications of the presence of painter nuns in the city is a letter (1634) written by Giulio Rospigliosi, the future Pope Clement IX, which mentions a young convent girl who painted an altarpiece for an altar in the church belonging to the convent of Spirito Santo. A few years later, the biographer Filippo Titi wrote that the nun had used a drawing by the famous painter Pietro da Cortona. Unfortunately, neither the subject represented, nor the identity of the artist are known. The painting was almost certainly moved from its altar in 1693 when Luigi Garzi was commissioned to execute a new altarpiece. It is impossible to determine whether other nuns also worked as artists here over the years. Certainly, the presence among the convent's surviving papers of some documents decorated with floral frames might suggest the work of the nuns themselves.

A better known and more studied example is the convent of San Giuseppe a Capo le Case, thanks first and foremost to the survival of the works executed by Sister Eufrasia Benedetti. These must have formed part of the programme of renewal following the canonization of St Teresa of Avila, who had established the Discalced Carmelites in Spain, and of Filippo Neri, instrumental in founding the Carmelite institution.

Sister Maria Eufrasia, born Flavia Benedetti (1597–1676), was the daughter of Lucia Paltrinieri and Andrea Benedetti, an expert embroiderer and art dealer. She entered the convent in 1628 after renouncing her inheritance. Already in 1638, Pompilio Totti wrote of some paintings executed by her for the adjacent church. His statement suggests that contemporaries considered these works to be out of the ordinary. We should not underestimate the importance of her friendship with the versatile artist Plautilla Bricci, who also worked with Flavia's brother Elpidio Benedetti. The two women artists met in around the 1630s, perhaps through the Carmelite friars who had commissioned Bricci to paint the altarpiece for the church of Santa Maria in Montesanto. Probably, despite the rules of seclusion, the two had the opportunity to meet in the locutory to discuss their faith and perhaps to debate artistic practice through the gratings and exchange objects through the wheel.

According to contemporary sources, Sister Eufrasia had executed paintings for the church of San Giuseppe, but the only ones to survive were on walls closed to the outside world, in spaces belonging to the sacristy of the church of San Giuseppe and the rooms of the former convent, which in 1980 became home to the modern art museum of the Municipality of Rome. These paintings stand out for their well-considered iconographical choices, symbolizing the transition from the worldly life of the exterior to the devout and penitent life of the convent thanks to the intercession of the Eucharistic miracle.

Dynamics of mutual support and dialogue in a cloistered environment can be traced in the history of the suppressed convent of Santa Maria dell'Umiltà. The institute was built at the behest of Francesca Baglioni Orsini, a significant figure in devotional patronage who chose to give away the inheritance left by her father and by her husband, who died in 1593 in Florence where the couple had lived for several years at the Medici court. Baglioni herself encouraged this flourishing of the arts, specifically choosing Chiara Alberti, daughter of the well-known artist Durante Alberti. Born on 19 May 1588, Chiara lived with her family at least until her father's death in 1614. On 13 April 1616, she made her religious profession and pronounced her vows. She had certainly already demonstrated her skills as a painter, honed at her home-workshop together with her brother Pierfrancesco: the inventory of Durante's properties describes as many as four paintings by her, though none are known today. Francesca Baglioni must have been aware of her work, perhaps through the mediation of Durante, who had worked for her cousin Alberto Baglioni.

In Santa Maria dell'Umiltà, the main activities practiced by the nuns included drawing, embroidery and weaving, in part for sale outside the convent. This information has re-emerged from the detailed account of life at the convent, offering fundamental evidence to better contextualize artistic culture within Roman convents. It is not yet possible to say whether such instances represent an

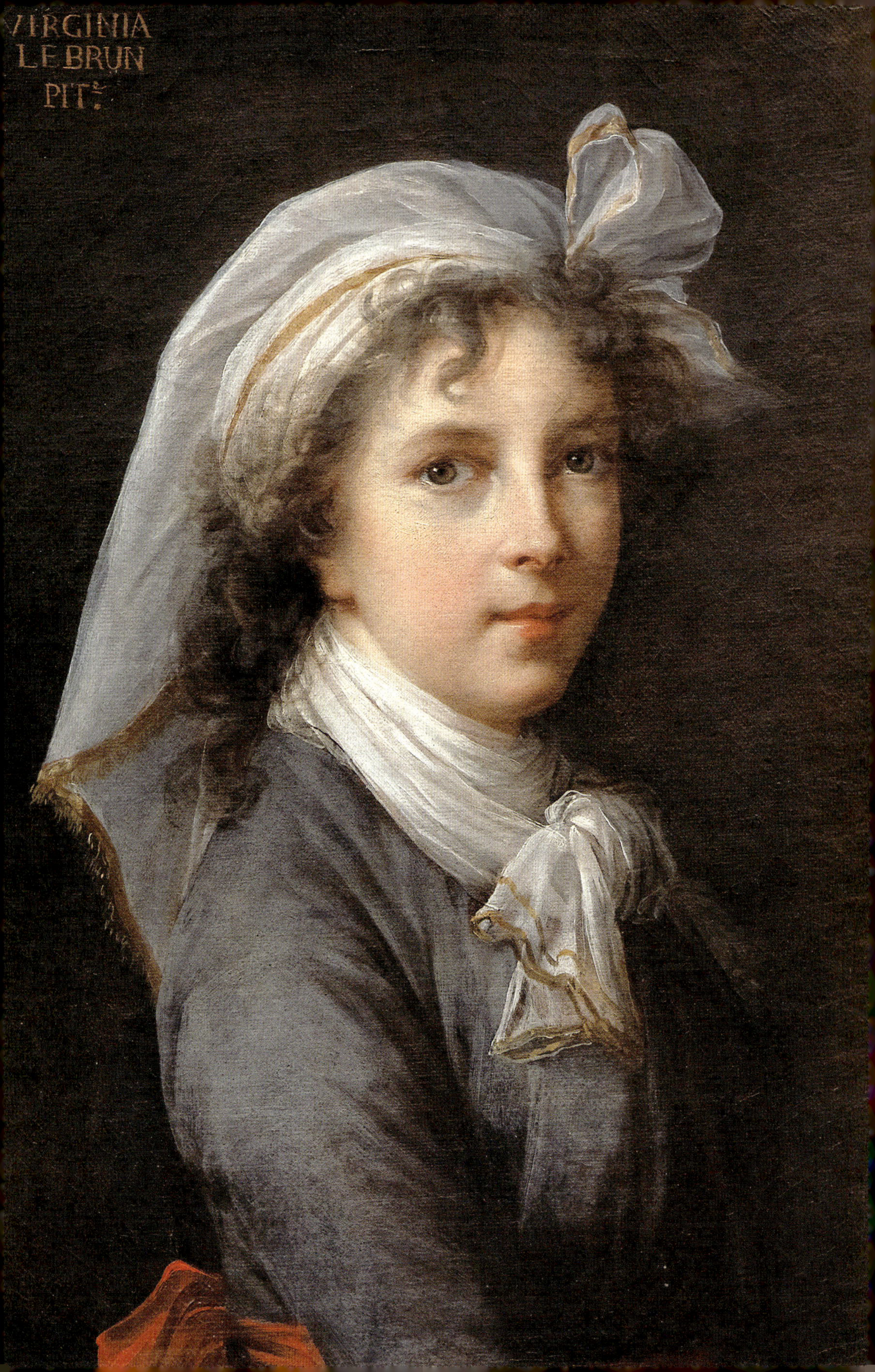
VIRGINIA
LE BRUN
PIT.

exception within the vast and wide-ranging phenomenon of monastic communities. The dispersal of many archives due to the closures suffered by these institutions over the centuries has led to the loss of extremely important sources as well as the works produced or commissioned for the interiors of convents.

From the Accademia di San Luca to the Arcadian Academy

Towards the end of the 17th century, when the Arcadian Academy was founded, the cultural climate in Rome was focused on the rediscovery of good taste, aspiring to establish a new social model in which women played an active and direct role. This cultural climate was favoured by the active presence in the city of Christina of Sweden. At the start of the new century, many Italian and foreign women artists settled in Rome, giving new impetus to the worlds of art and literature with their entry into the Arcadian Academy and the Accademia di San Luca, which continued to play a leading role.

One of the first members of the Arcadian Academy, already in 1704, was Faustina Maratti. After initially working as a painter, she abandoned the brush for the pen and devoted herself to her passion for poetry. The daughter of Carlo Maratti, one of the most acclaimed artists of his time, she learned the first rudiments of drawing thanks to her father's teachings. She was appreciated for her eloquence to the extent that she was considered a source of inspiration by her contemporaries. An example is the portrait in the Pinacoteca civica "F. Podesti" in Ancona, which, though a work of fantasy, presents her as a fashionable lady holding a manuscript composition and the inscription "Faustina Maratti painter and poetess". Her many talents allowed her to shine not for her family origins but for her writings, distinguishing herself among Roman intellectuals as a woman author. After her, other women painters also entered the academy: Maria Felice Tibaldi (1749), Caterina Cherubini (1766) and Marianna Candidi.

The Grand Tour: Rome and the Miniaturists

Between the 18th and 19th centuries, many women miniaturists graced the Roman market with their creations, particularly sought after by Grand Tourists. Maria Felice Tibaldi's talent was celebrated by her contemporaries, who wrote that already by the age of twelve she was supporting her family financially. Over the course of her career, she experimented with small-format copies of works by the most famous artists, including those of Pierre Subleyras whom she married in 1739, successfully introducing him to Roman patrons. One of the most important recognitions came in 1752 when her copy of the *Dinner at the House of Simon the Pharisee* became the first painting by a living artist to be purchased for the Capitoline collection (where it can still be found today). According to the sources, Tibaldi also painted in oils; proof of this can be found in her portrait by Subleyras (now in the Worcester Art Museum), where a medium-sized canvas with a figure in a melancholic pose is visible in the middle ground. Maria Felice's legacy was continued by her sister Teresa and daughter Clementina.

Caterina Cherubini's miniatures were also highly sought-after. She specialized in executing small works on copper, copies or inventions inspired by Bolognese and Roman classicism. After marrying her teacher Francisco Preciado de La Vaga, Cherubini travelled with him from Italy to Spain, becoming a member of both the Accademia di San Luca and the Academia de San Fernando (Madrid) between 1760 and 1761.

Therese Concordia Mengs was another specialist in this art, attaining the prestigious position of court miniaturist in Dresden in 1745, after living for a few years in Rome. She returned to the city in her forties and married the painter Anton Von Maron. After her admission to the Accademia di San Luca, she opened a studio-school attended by many women artists, including Marianna Waldestein from Vienna and Sofia Clerk from Turin.

Élisabeth Vigée (Le Brun), *Self-Portrait*, 1790. Rome, Accademia Nazionale di San Luca.

Foreign Artists in Rome Between the 17th and 19th Centuries: Kauffmann, Vigée, Seidler

Angelika Kauffmann was a key figure in the establishment of the woman artist between the 18th and 19th centuries: she aspired to become a history painter, working in a genre reserved for men. Despite various personal difficulties, she persevered and in 1781 married the painter Antonio Zucchi, moving with him to Rome. Here she built up her reputation as a cultured and cosmopolitan artist, obtaining equal pay with her male colleagues.

In Rome, Kauffmann acquired a studio in Via Sistina that became an intellectual meeting place, frequented by figures like Johann Wolfgang von Goethe. With a production of over a thousand works, Angelika broke the mould of traditional techniques and became a model for other women artists. She played a fundamental role in the rebirth of the Italian school, acknowledged for her unique style at a time when there were no great masters. On her death in 1807, the famous sculptor Antonio Canova organised her funeral, attended by the whole intellectual community of Rome, and her bust was placed in the Pantheon.

The French artist Élisabeth Vigée was a great admirer of Kauffmann, whom she knew and frequented after arriving in Rome in November 1789. During her stay, she executed numerous portraits of cosmopolitan figures, including Countess Anna Potocka and Madame Victoire de France. She exhibited a self-portrait at the Académie de France and in 1790 was elected member of the Accademia di San Luca.

Another important foreign woman artist in Rome was Luise Seidler, who settled here from 1818, helping to disseminate the neo-medieval style and joining the German-Scandinavian community. Seidler painted portraits of prominent individuals like the actress Fanny Caspers and collaborated with other artists, working together on paintings. She assembled around her a group of women intellectuals who played an active role in the city's cultural life, thus significantly helping to consolidate the status of women artists in Rome.

The 19th Century: Stabilizing the Role of Female Artists

The presence of foreign women artists in Rome gave new visibility to women, who began to make room for themselves in the Roman art system in the early 19th century despite difficulties and discrimination. The Academies of Fine Arts, institutionalized by the Napoleonic government, admitted female artists as students, though with some differences with respect to their male colleagues.

A significant example was Carlotta Gargalli, the first woman student at the Reale Accademia di Belle Arti in Bologna. From 1804 to 1807, Carlotta received an excellent education and in 1811 obtained a special permit through Canova to enter the Accademia d'Italia in Rome. The commission judged her suited to a career as a copyist, but the training she completed in the city allowed her to demonstrate more advanced skills. At the end of her time in Rome, she executed the large painting of *Pyrrhus Threatening Andromache to Kill Her Son Astyanax*, thus encroaching on history painting. After returning to Bologna, she became one of the most sought-after women artists, abreast of current international styles.

Bianca Milesi, another prominent woman artist, was influenced by the Milanese salon of her mother Elena Visconti and became a student of renowned masters such as Giuseppe Bossi and Andrea Appiani linked to the Accademia di Belle Arti di Brera. Her career began with an important commission in Rome, where she became established in the art world thanks to her skills as a portraitist. Milesi forged meaningful ties with other artists, like the German Sophie Reinhard, with whom she shared her experiences and travels, thus helping to create a support network among women in the arts.

Over the following years, the art scene in Rome was further enriched. The international exhibitions held on the Capitoline in 1809 and 1810, inspired by Parisian models, were key to the visibility of women artists. At the first exhibition, six women displayed their works, including Rosa Mezzera and Hortense Lescot, the latter winning a prize for her painting *The Pipers*. Lescot had been in Rome since 1807 and had strong ties to Canova; her work privileged folk themes, reflecting the artistic trends of the time. The exhibition of 1810 marked a further step forward, with eight women artists among the fifty-nine participants. Their works ranged from landscapes to portraits and sculptures, showing the diversity of women's talents. The women artists, such as Matilde Meoni and Anna Diamanti, tackled different themes, enriching the Roman art world.

Despite their progress, women artists faced a difficult path. Opportunities for public visibility remained limited and their presence in the art world was often seen as secondary with respect to men. However, they did begin to gain recognition: through talent and hard work they managed to defy conventions, paving the way for future generations of women in the arts.

In 1823, sixteen women artists were admitted to the Congregazione del Pantheon, recognized for their talent as well as their faith. Among them were Marianna Candidi, Giulia Massimo, Rosa Mezzera and in the following years Ida Botti, Matilde Meoni and Amalia De Angelis, the first to win the Gregorian Competition in 1845. Artists such as Camilla Guiscardi distinguished themselves at exhibitions in Turin and Rome. From 1839, many participated in group exhibitions in Piazza del Popolo, consolidating their presence in the Roman art world.

This cultural climate was crucial to the training of Emma Gaggiotti a Roman painter who is almost forgotten today but who was acclaimed throughout the 19th century at the greatest courts of Europe. A student of Tommaso Minardi, she lived between Rome and Ancona, becoming a fervent patriot and actively fundraising for Risorgimento causes. Emma achieved great popularity in London, where her paintings, inspired by Raphael, caught the attention of Prince Albert. In 1851, she exhibited a self-portrait at the Royal Academy, a copy of which was later commissioned by Queen Victoria for her husband. The future Prussian king William I also took an interest in her, even becoming her principal patron; thanks to his support, the painter received numerous commissions, including a portrait for Napoleon III. In the 1850s, Emma moved to Berlin, where she portrayed numerous famous people. Following the death of William I in 1888, she lost favour with the court and spent the last years of her life between Rome and Velletri, surrounded by her rich collection and away from the spotlight.

Rome continued to be an important centre of artistic work and training during the modern period, emerging as a cosmopolitan city capable of attracting a growing number of women artists, both Italian and foreign. These women had the opportunity to work more freely, sharing studios and interests with male colleagues. Although the gradual reduction in major aristocratic commissions made it impossible to maintain an art scene like that engendered by the great 19th century international exhibitions of France and England, the future capital of Italy nonetheless confirmed its status as a hub of artistic innovation.

General Bibliography

Linda Nochlin, "Why have there been no great women artists?" *ARTnews* (1971), 22–39.

Women Artists: 1550–1950, exhib. cat. (Los Angeles–Pittsburgh–Brooklyn 1976–77), ed. by Ann Sutherland Harris, Linda Nochlin. New York: Knopf, 1976.

Anna Banti, *Quando anche le donne si misero a dipingere*. Milan: La tartaruga, 1982; 2nd ed. Milan: Abscondita, 2011.

Franca Trinchieri Camiz, "Virgo-non sterilis... Nuns as Artists in Seventeenth-Century Rome." In *Picturing Women in Renaissance and Baroque Italy*, ed. by Geraldine A. Johnson, Sara F. Matthews Grieco. Cambridge: Cambridge University Press, 1997, 139–64.

Simona Feci, *Pesci fuor d'acqua: donne a Roma in età moderna: diritti e patrimoni*. Rome: Viella, 2004.

Susanne Adina Meyer, "Le mostre in Campidoglio durante il periodo napoleonico." In *Fictions of Isolation: Artistic and Intellectual Exchange in Rome During the First Half of the Nineteenth Century*, ed. by Lorenz Enderlein, Nino Zchomelidse. Rome: L'Erma di Bretschneider, 2006, 29–47.

Julia Vicioso, *Costanza Francini tra Artemisia Gentileschi e le committenze della Compagnia della Pietà in San Giovanni dei Fiorentini a Roma*. Rome: GBE Bentivoglio, 2014.

Sylke Kaufmann, *Louise Seidler (1786-1866) – Leben und Werk: mit einem Œuvreverzeichnis ihrer Ölgemälde, Pastelle und bildmäßigen Zeichnungen*. 2 vols. Bucha bei Jena: Quartus-Verlag, 2016.

Le donne nel cantiere di San Pietro in Vaticano. Artiste, artigiane e imprenditrici dal XVI al XIX secolo, ed. by Assunta Di Sante, Simona Turriziani. Foligno: Il Formichiere, 2017.

La grandezza dell'universo nell'arte di Giovanna Garzoni, catalogo della mostra (Florence 2020), ed. by Sheila Barker. Leghorn: Sillabe, 2020.

Le Signore dell'Arte. Storie di donne tra '500 e '600, exhib. cat. (Milan 2021), ed. by Annamaria Bava, Gioia Mori, Alain Tapié. Milan: Skira, 2021.

Caravaggio e Artemisia. La sfida di Giuditta: violenza e seduzione nella pittura tra Cinque e Seicento, exhib. cat. (Rome 2021–22), ed. by Maria Cristina Terzaghi. Rome: Officina Libraria, 2021.

Carlotta Gargalli 1788-1840. Una pittrice bolognese nella Roma di Canova, exhib. cat. (Bologna 2023), ed. by Ilaria Chia, Francesca Sinigaglia. Bologna: MiG, 2023.

Now You See Us. Women Artists in Britain 1520–1920, exhib. cat. (London 2024), ed. by Tabitha Barber. London: Tate, 2024.

Pierre-François Eugène Giraud, ***Portrait of Mathilde Bonaparte While Painting***, c. 1850. Rome, Museo Napoleonico.

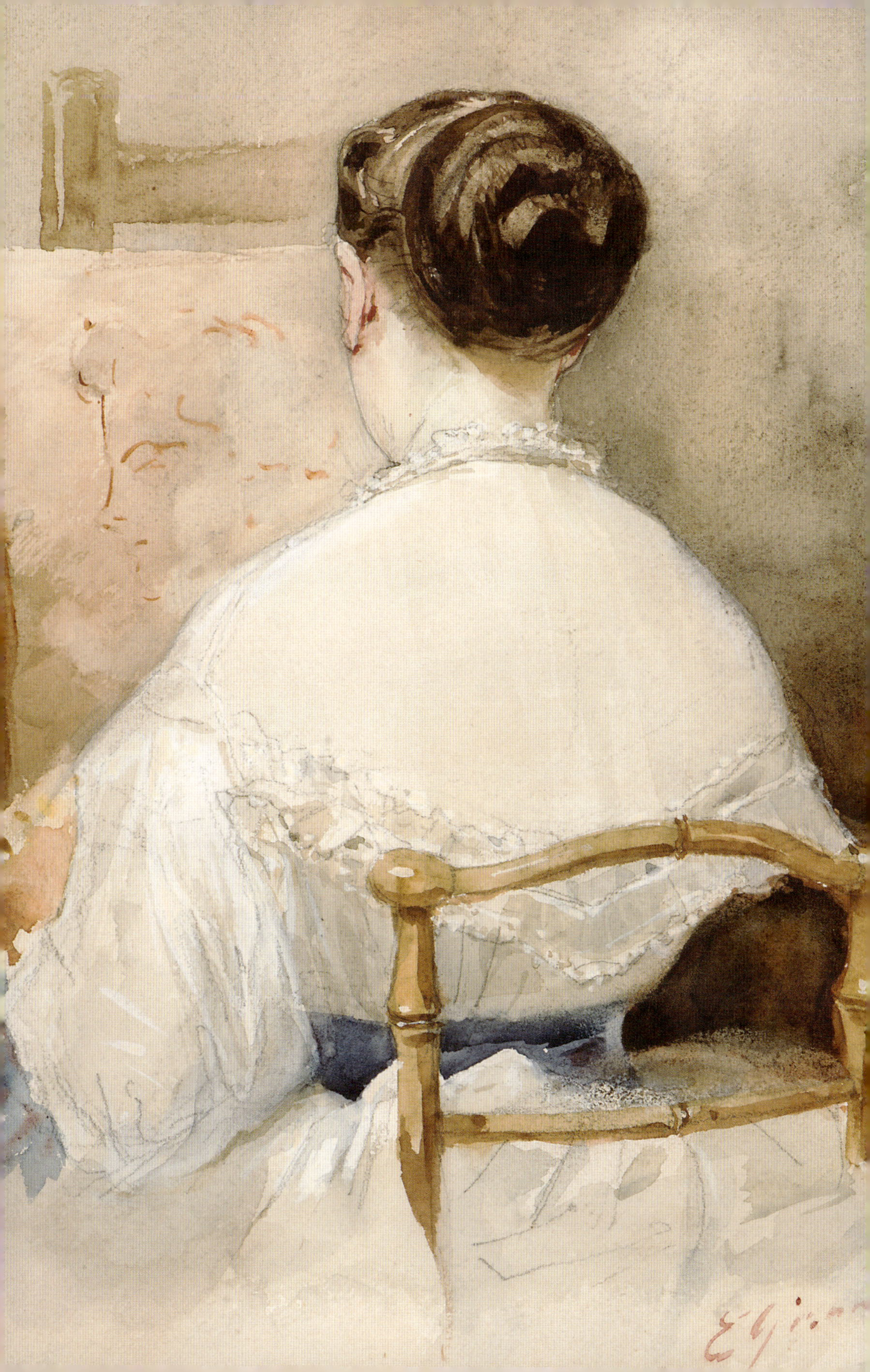

BIOGRAPHIES

The women artists are presented here in alphabetical order by their maiden names; where relevant their married name, often better known, is also given. Some of the women artists included have been studied in depth here for the first time while for others further archive research has led to new discoveries. The biographies thus reconstructed, focusing exclusively on their work in Rome, are accompanied by an essential reference bibliography. Each artist is accompanied by an image depicting one of her most important paintings or a work in which she is portrayed.

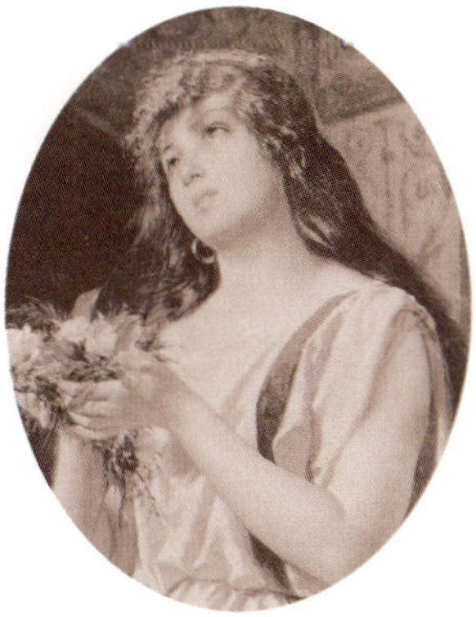

Virginia Barlocci (Riccardi; Mariani)

(Rome, 1824–1898)

Virginia was a Roman painter and ceramicist, the student of the Purist painter from Parma Bernardino Riccardi (Parma, 1814 – Rome, 1854), whom she married in 1854, just over a month before his death in October of the same year. To her husband the painter dedicated a funerary memorial still in the church of Santa Maria sopra Minerva in Rome. In 1861 she participated in the *Esposizione italiana* in Florence with six works entered in category XXIII: Painting, Engraving, Drawings and Lithographs. In the *Guida di Roma* published by Alessandro Rufini in the same year, we learn that she worked as a teacher "of watercolour painting – Piazza di Santa Chiara no. 49, third floor", while on 6 November 1862 she was appointed member of the Congregazione dei Virtuosi al Pantheon and in 1879 of the Accademia di San Luca. The painter was an active participant in the artistic life of Rome, displaying on several occasions at the annual exhibitions of the Società degli amatori e cultori delle belle arti of Rome. In 1864 the *Giornale di Roma* noted that "a little painting by Signora Barlocci was also admired; she is one of the most distinguished members of the fairer sex who grace the arts in Rome". The artist is also mentioned in the catalogue of the *Esposizione internazionale di belle arti* held in Rome in 1883, on which occasion she exhibited in her dual capacity as painter and ceramicist. The private collection of the artist Cesare Mariani, the painter's husband from 1863, formerly included two of the works later acquired for the collections of the Museo di Roma (inv. MR 20706; MR 20709) .

BIBLIOGRAPHY: Anna Lisa Genovese, "Diario 1852–1877." In Vitaliano Tiberia, *La Congregazione dei Virtuosi al Pantheon da Pio VII a Pio IX*. Galatina: Congedo, 2015, 777; Angelo De Gubernatis, s.v. *Dizionario degli artisti italiani viventi. Pittori, scultori e architetti*. Florence: Le Monnier, 1889, 281.

Michela D'Agostino

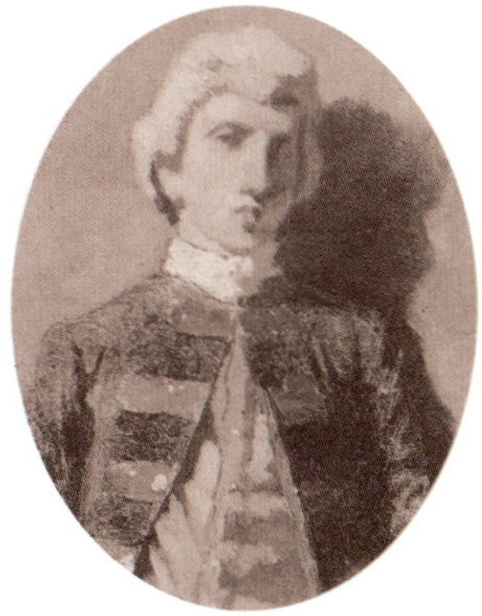

Jane Benham (Hay)

(London, 1829 – Brussels, 1904)

An important Pre-Raphaelite artist, Jane Benham was active in Italy in the second half of the 19th century. She first trained in London with William Riviere and then with Wilhelm von Kaulbach in Munich, where she had travelled with her friend, the painter Anna Mary Howitt. After marrying the artist William Milton Hay, she settled in Paris in 1852. Here she met Saverio Altamura who became her life partner after 1855, the year of her move to Florence. In the Tuscan city, Jane was an active participant in the art world, displaying at the exhibitions of the Promotrice delle Belle Arti, a society for the promotion of the arts, and at the studio she shared with Altamura in Via del Mugnone. Probably towards the end of the 1850s Benham travelled to Rome, a fundamental destination for artists, as attested by the small oil on cardboard in the Museo di Roma, depicting a *Male Figure in Eighteenth-Century Clothes* (inv. MR 44979), and the painting with a *Roman Costume* presented at the Promotrice of 1860; on the same occasion Altamura displayed the *Remnant of a Roman Aqueduct*. These subjects clearly reflect the experiments undertaken during their stay in Rome, aimed at the study of local costumes and, both here and in Tuscany, of the landscape. The time spent in Italy and her relationship with Altamura were fundamental in the artist's career. In addition to gaining a deeper knowledge of 15th and 16th century art, she turned her hand to the practice of *plein-air* painting: the letters of Barbara Bod-

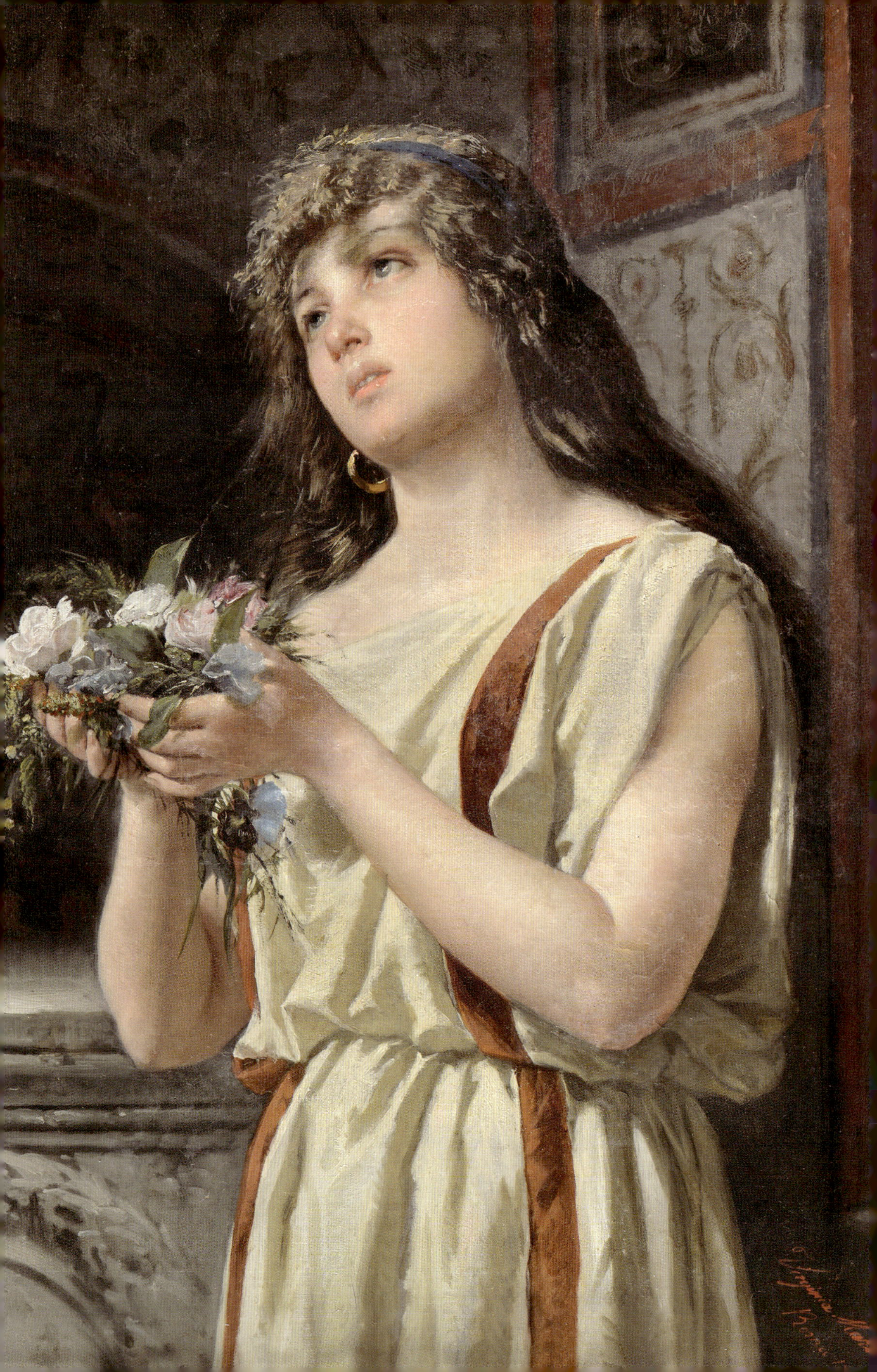

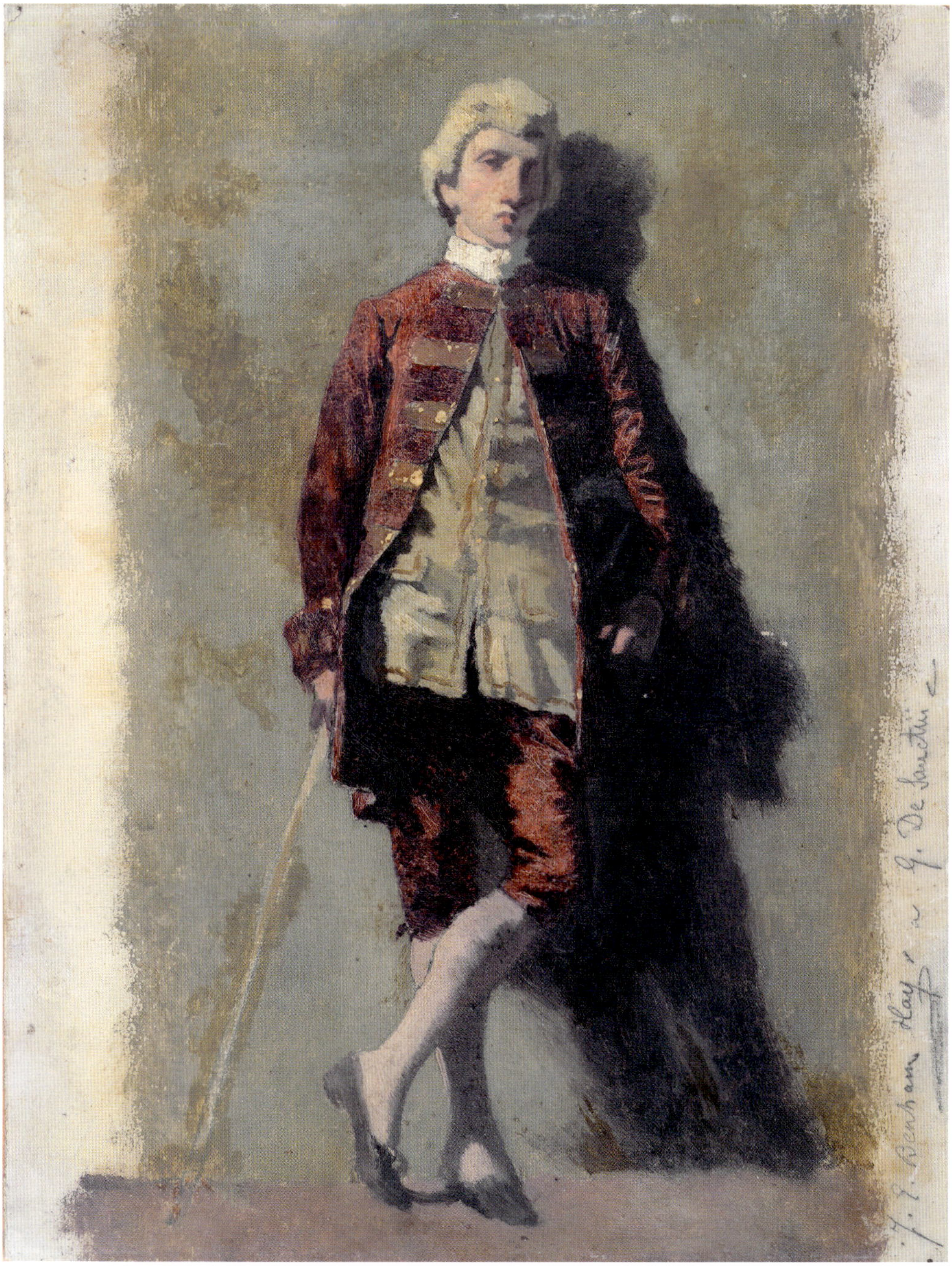

Virginia Barlocci (Riccardi; Mariani), *Young Girl Offering Flowers in Pompeian Attire*, 1884. Rome, Museo di Roma.

Jane Benham (Hay), *Male Figure in Eighteenth-Century Clothes*, c. 1860. Rome, Museo di Roma.

ichon and the pages on Florence of Elihu Vedder's autobiography describe whole days spent painting in the countryside. This practice helped her to develop an original and personal Pre-Raphaelism, updated in light of the research of the Macchiaioli and the Purists, clearly apparent in her most famous works: *England and Italy* (1859, private collection), a manifesto of her adherence to the Risorgimento cause, and the monumental canvas *A Florentine Procession* (Cambridge, Homerton College). In around 1867 she moved to Naples, presumably with Altamura, and became an assiduous presence at the exhibitions of the Società Promotrice between 1871 and 1873.

The last information on the painter's activity concerns the execution of a work depicting a *Venetian Procession* and her relations with the English patrons present in Venice, to whom she sent works until 1877.

BIBLIOGRAPHY: Annabel Robinson, John Purkis, Ann Massing, *A Florentine Procession: A Painting by Jane Benham Hay at Homerton College*. Cambridge: Homestead Press, 1997; Susanna Tornesello, "Jane E. Benham Hay: una pittrice preraffaellita a Firenze negli anni del Caffè Michelangelo." *Antologia Vieusseux* new ser. 14, no. 40 (2008), 49–71.

Jessica Calipari

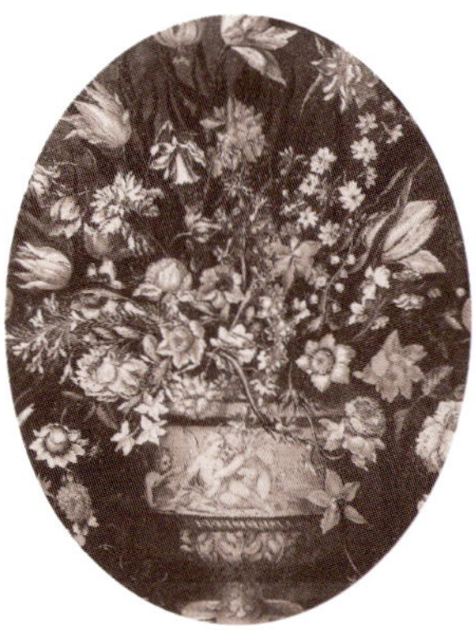

Laura Bernasconi, also called Laura dei Fiori

(Rome, second half of the 17th century)

Laura Bernasconi is known thanks to various biographers, including Filippo Titi and Lione Pascoli, who mentioned her execution of a frame of flowers for an altarpiece (now lost) dedicated to St Cajetan and executed in 1629 by Andrea Camassei for the church of Sant'Andrea della Valle in Rome. Her name also appears in some inventories of important Roman collections: four paintings in the Doria-Pamphilj collection (inv. FC 679, FC 680, FC 681, FC 682) have been attributed to her thanks to the precise descriptions in the 1725 inventory, which also include the dimensions. She is known to have trained under Mario Nuzzi, called Mario dei Fiori, whose nickname she also acquired. It has not yet been established exactly when she attended his workshop, but Pascoli considers her the student who more than any other made "good use of his teachings, and of the love and the manner in which he imparted them" (p. 509). The market price of her paintings also suggests that she was well-established and appreciated by her contemporaries. In the accounts book of the merchant Pellegrino Peri, it is noted that in 1673 he sold to the silversmith Pietro Paolo Bezzi three paintings on glass for one *scudo* and eighty *baiocchi*, and four of her tondos with flowers were valued at eighteen *scudi* by Giuseppe Ghezzi. Though her name has not yet been found in the parish registers, numerous members of the Bernasconi family – a common last name in 17th century Rome – are recorded in the parish of Santa Maria del Popolo. Today, various paintings are attributed to her (many of which have appeared on the art market) on the basis of a stylistic analysis. In publicly owned collections we could mention, as attributed to her, the *Vase of Flowers* now in the Museo Civico di Sarnico. In the 19th century she was also credited with some landscapes in the Musée des Beaux-Arts of Bordeaux (inv. M.5714, M.6156), suggesting a more complex training in Nuzzi's workshop; according to the studies he may also have worked in other genres such as portraiture and – significantly – landscape painting. It is also important to draw attention to her work as a fresco painter on the decoration of the ceiling of the Galleria Colonna, alongside Giovanni Paolo and Filippo Schor, where she should probably be credited with the execution of the trophies and standards.

BIBLIOGRAPHY: Loredana Lorizzo, "Pittori di natura morta e mercato dell'arte nella Roma del Seicento: novità su Andrea Bonanni, Carlo Manieri, Antonio Tibaldi, Giovan Battista Gavarotti e Laura Bernasconi." In *Natura morta: rappresentazione dell'oggetto, oggetto come rappresentazione*, ed. by Costanza Barbieri, Dalma Frascarelli. Naples: Arte'm, 2010, 94; Andrea G. De Marchi, *Collezione Doria Pamphilj. Catalogo generale dei dipinti*. Cinisello Balsamo: Silvana, 2016, 53–4.

Ilaria Arcangeli

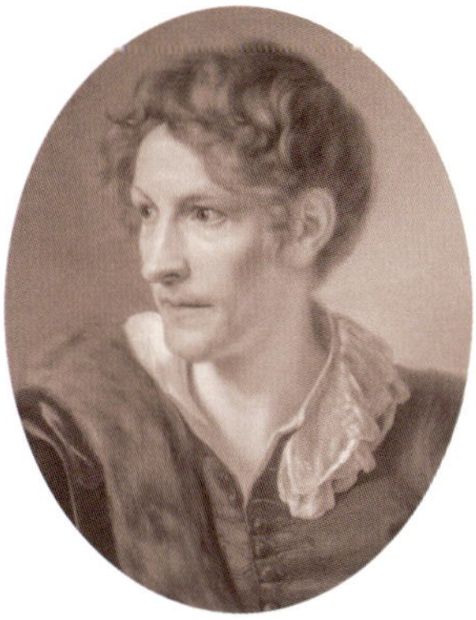

Luisa Bersani

(Rome, 1808/09–1888)

Luisa Bersani belonged to the affluent Roman middle class. Though unconnected to the art world, her father Giacomo spent large amounts of money to ensure that his daughter was "taught literature and painting by carefully selected masters", as noted when his estate was divided up in 1851. She was accepted into the school of Vincenzo Camuccini (1771–1844), where she received an education based on Canova's Neoclassical style. At the age of only eighteen, Luisa gave the Accademia di San Luca a portrait of its director Bertel Thorvaldsen (inv. 186), a copy after Camuccini, which was immediately placed alongside other portraits of the Accademia's professors. Given the high quality of the painting, on 10 June 1827 Luisa was admitted to the Accademia as an honorary member at the suggestion of the president himself. From the documents uncovered, we learn that from 1830, and for at least twenty years, her workshop was located in Via del Corso no. 202, in an apartment of her father's house. In the list drawn up by Keller as a guide to collectors, she is described as a "history and portrait painter". The inventory of her studio mentions some still life oil paintings, while the presence of some plaster busts is evidence of the practice of using sculptures as models for her paintings. In 1832, on the proposal of Luigi Durantini and after a unanimous vote, Luisa Bersani was elected a member of the Congregazione dei Virtuosi al Pantheon. In addition to the aforementioned portrait of Thorvaldsen, the Istituto Centrale per la Grafica possesses two prints based on the painter's drawings: *The Blessed Humbert of Savoy* by Giovanni Battista Balestra (inv. S-FC51025) and *The Blessed Boniface of Savoy, Archbishop of Canterbury* by Ignazio Pavon (inv. S-FC51299). By contrast, the fate of her paintings, known thanks to the 1842 inventory of her property, remains obscure. Luisa Bersani died unmarried in Rome in 1888, long after a broken arm had forced her to give up painting.

BIBLIOGRAPHY: Vitaliano Tiberia, *La Congregazione dei Virtuosi al Pantheon da Pio VII a Pio IX*. Galatina: Congedo, 2015, 62, 75, 293, 294, nos. 240, 295, 899.

Sofya Utvenko

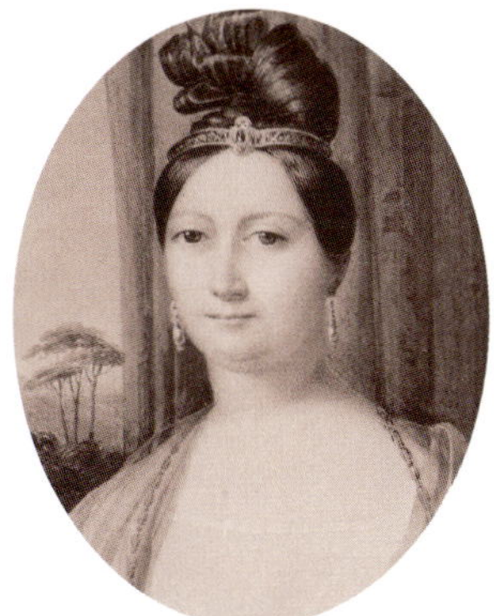

Charlotte Bonaparte

(Mortefontaine, Oise, 1802 – Sarzana, 1839)

Charlotte was the second child of Joseph Bonaparte (1768–1844), Napoleon's older brother and king of Naples (1806–1808) and Spain (1808–1813), and of Julie Clary. An amateur draughtswoman and engraver, she studied the graphic arts and painting like many women of the Bonaparte family, and demonstrated a talent for landscape painting in watercolour. Exiled from France (1814–1824), she spent her childhood and adolescence between Europe and North America. While in Brussels from 1820 to 1821 she was a student of the famous painter Jacques-Louis David alongside her cousin Juliette de Villeneuve and Teresa Cabarrus, in an environment that encouraged women to train in the arts. In 1824 she travelled to Rome to marry her cousin Napoléon-Louis Bonaparte, hosted by *Madame Mère* Maria Letizia Ramolino at her residence in Piazza Venezia and country estate in Via San Paolo at Albano. After a long stay here, she married in Florence in 1826. Though officially living with her husband in Palazzo Gianfigliazzi and later in Palazzo Serristori, she continued to travel frequently to Rome to see her beloved sister Zénaïde, staying

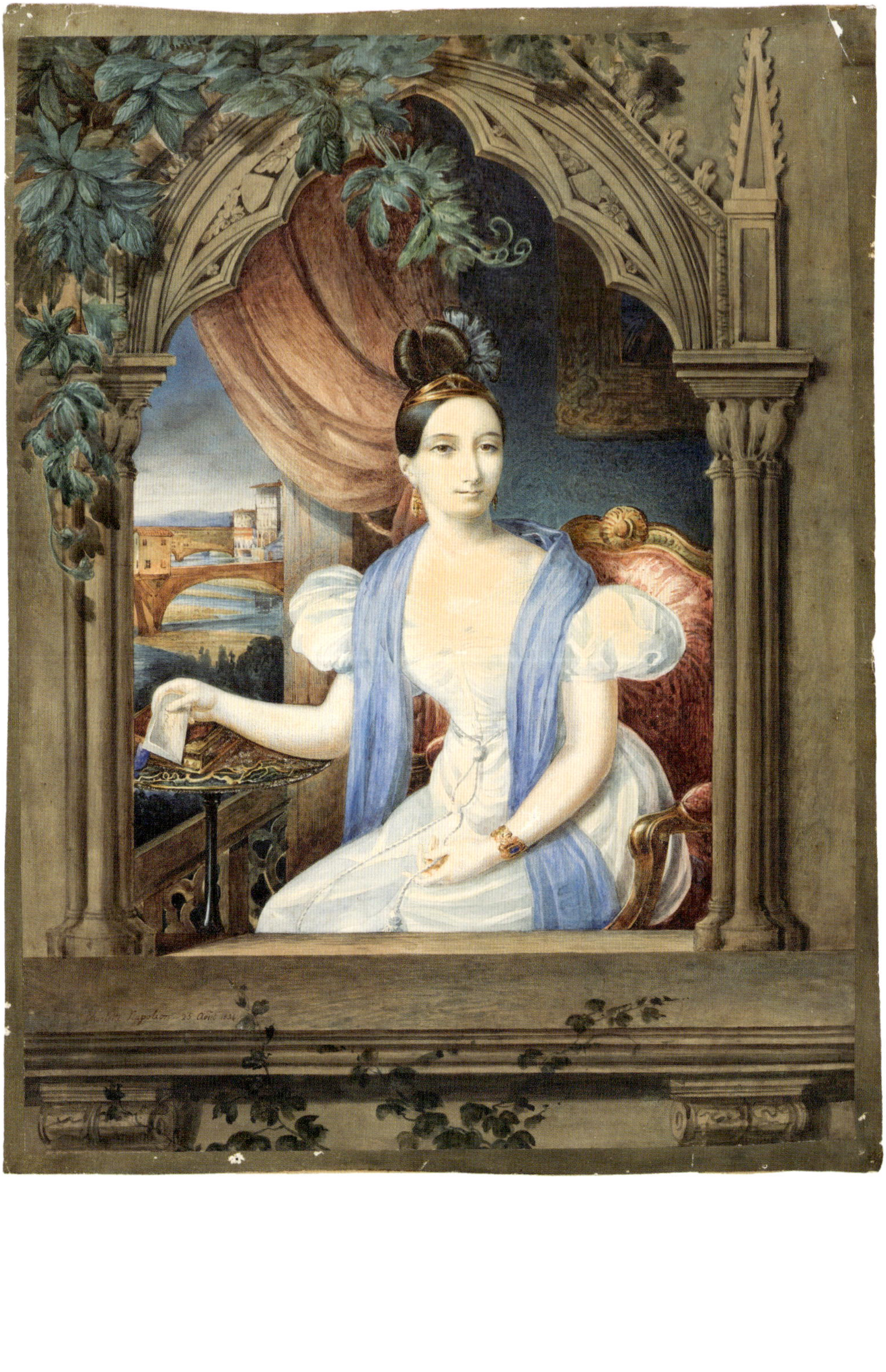

Charlotte Bonaparte, *Self-Portrait*, 1834. Rome, Museo Napoleonico.

Mathilde Létizia Wilhelmine Bonaparte, *Portrait of a Woman*, 1883. Rome, Museo Napoleonico.

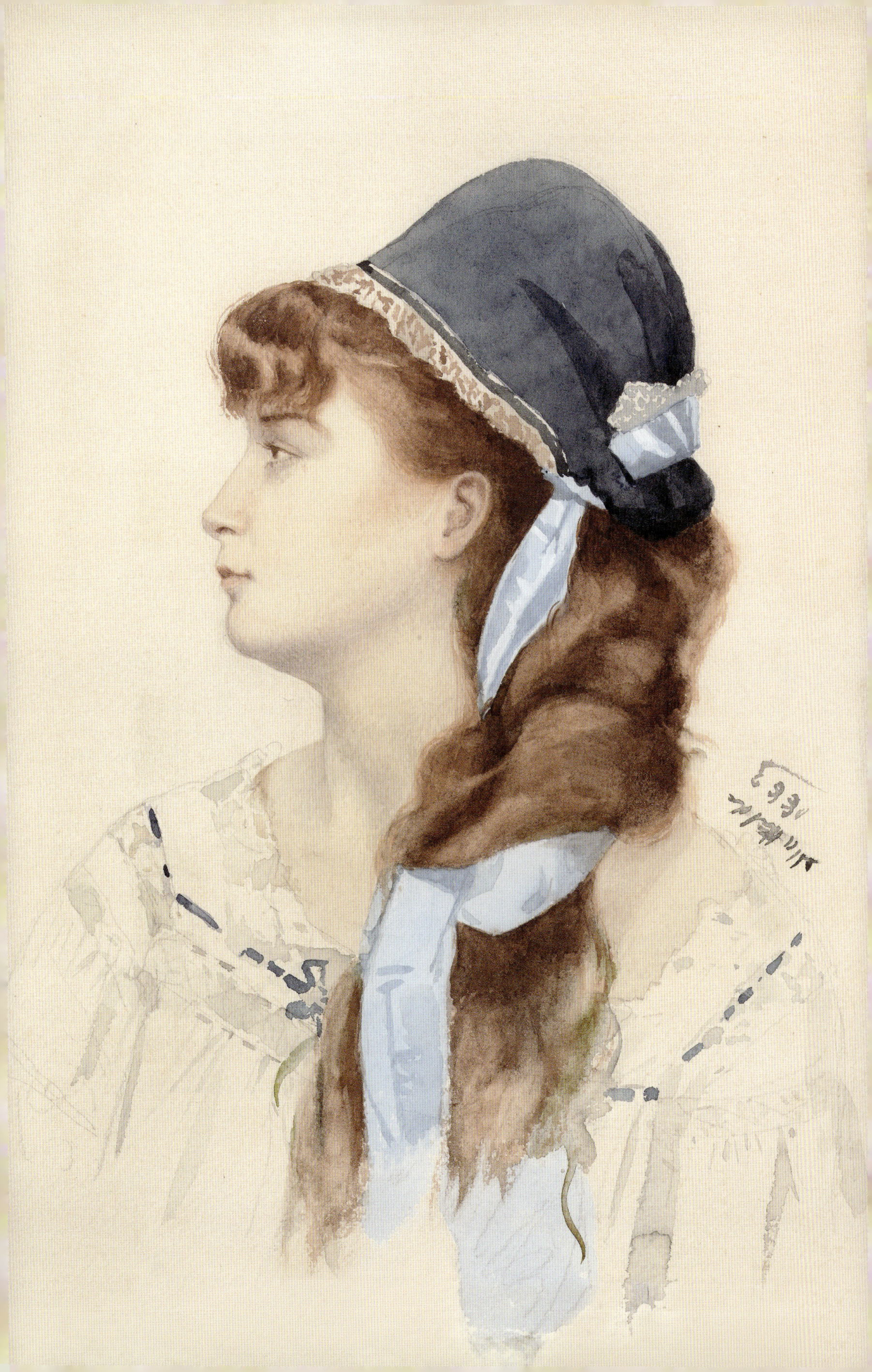

at Villa Paolina on the Via Nomentana where she lived (see the drawing of the living room in Villa Paolina attributed to Jodocus Sebastien Van den Abeele, Rome, Museo Napoleonico, inv. MN 500). From 1838 she settled in Rome to distance herself from the rumours about her presumed affairs after the premature death of her husband in 1831. From her earliest stays in the 1820s she executed various watercolours of the Roman countryside (Rome, Museo Napoleonico, album inv. MN 969), in addition to portraits of family members, like that of her grandmother Letizia of 1835 (Rome, Museo Napoleonico, inv. MN 959). She also met a number of prominent figures, such as Alessandro Capalti, a student of Tommaso Minardi, who intervened on various drawings by Bonaparte (Rome, Museo Napoleonico, album inv. MN 7804) including the aforementioned portrait of *Madame Mère* in the Museo Napoleonico in Rome. Other acquaintances included Samuel Jesi and Léopold Robert, from whom she learned the technique of engraving, Bartolomeo Pinelli and his son Achille, whom she described as "the little Pinelli", Franz Ludwig Catel and many others. Her travels can be reconstructed thanks to the information provided by the numerous letters she exchanged with her family members and their correspondence with each other, cited in detail in the catalogue of the exhibition *Charlotte Bonaparte* (held in Rome in 2010 at the Museo Napoleonico), most of which had already been published by Piero Misciattelli in 1936. One of 1826, for example, describes her first contacts with the Roman art world. Another source of help in reconstructing her relations with artists working in Rome and Florence is her *Carnet de dépenses* of the years 1835–1838.

BIBLIOGRAPHY: *Charlotte Bonaparte, dama di molto spirito. La romantica vita di una principessa artista*, exhib. cat. (Rome 2010), ed. by Giulia Gorgone, Maria Elisa Tittoni. Leghorn: Sillabe, 2010.

Virginia Spadaccini

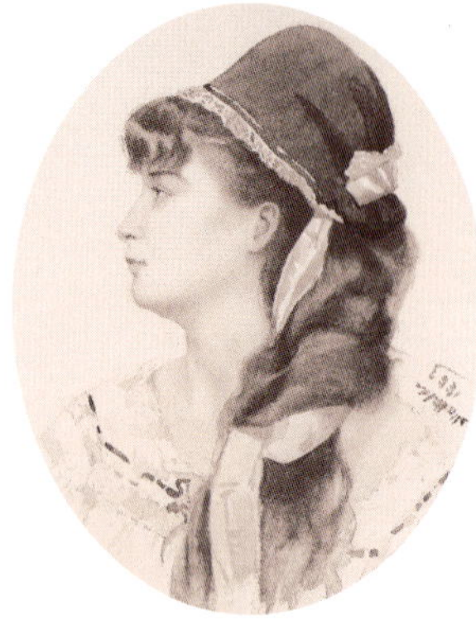

Mathilde Létizia Wilhelmine Bonaparte

(Trieste, 1820 – Paris, 1904)

An artist, patron, collector and celebrated *salonnière*, Mathilde Létizia Wilhelmine Bonaparte, nicknamed *Notre-Dame des arts* by her contemporaries, was born in Trieste on 27 May 1820. Her parents were Jérôme Bonaparte and Catharina of Württemberg, formerly the reigning couple of Westphalia, exiled to Italy after the fall of the Napoleonic empire. The niece of Czar Alexander I and of Napoleon, the young royal spent her childhood in Rome, where the family lived stably from 1823 to 1830 in Palazzo Núñez. She made almost daily visits to *Madame Mère* Maria Letizia Ramolino in Palazzo Rinuccini together with her uncle, Cardinal Joseph Fesch, and also frequented the library at Palazzo Falconieri where she took piano and writing lessons and visited her aunt Hortense at Villa Paolina. In 1830 the Bonapartist circle was disbanded, forced to leave the city after being accused of participating in the Carbonari uprisings, and Mathilde moved to Florence with her family in 1831, settling in Palazzo Serristori. Introduced to the arts already when very young at the Württemberg court, where she had studied music, singing and embroidery as was customary for aristocratic women of her rank and in particular of her family, she was particularly fond of painting and trained with Michel Ghislain Stapleaux (1799–1881). In Florence she specialized in drawing and watercolour painting, frequenting the circle of Neoclassical artists active in the city, Pietro Tenerani (1789–1869) and Lorenzo Bartolini (1777–1850), and continued to take painting lessons from Ida Botti Scifoni (1812–1844). These youthful years shaped her taste as a painter and collector: from Florence, Mathilde made numerous visits to Rome, the first already in 1833. While staying in the city's Napoleonic residences she took daily walks around all of Rome's museums and artists' studios. In 1840 she reluctantly left the city after marrying Prince Anatole Demidov and moved to the luxurious villa at San Donato, where she remained until her separation from her husband and definitive departure for Paris in 1846. In the French capital she studied painting under the guidance of Ernest Hébert (1817–1908) and Eugène Giraud (1806–1881); the latter later became one of her most trusted friends and a constant presence at the princess's famous salon, hosted in her city residence in Rue de Courcelles and in her country house at Saint-Gratien. This was a meeting place for the most progressive intellectuals, writers and scholars, also frequented by the sculptor Émilien de Nieuwerkerke, who was engaged in a love affair with the princess and became Intendant des Beaux-Arts under Napoleon III thanks to her influence. From 1857 she displayed at the *Salon*, until 1863 in the painting section and from 1864 in the graphic arts section, winning some medals. Of her the pro-imperialist press said that "she loves and understands the arts better than anyone". Her style was appreciated for its masculine qualities – as in the famous recollection by Charles-Augustin de Sainte-Beuve: "Her style has nothing small or fussy about it, nor that betrays the hand of a woman; rather, one might think oneself before one the works of a talented young man practicing with a generous spirit and developing his skill" – just like her conversation. Her cousin Julie del Gallo di Roccagiovine Bonaparte wrote in her memoirs that Mathilde was "in great demand [...] among serious men, because her conversation, substantial or even virile, is to their taste". In the words of the Goncourt brothers, her salon was "the true salon of the 19th century, with a lady of the house who is the perfect model of a modern woman [...] the woman artist, something very different from what was called a 'virtuosa' in the 18th century". Finally, as well as being a talented watercolourist, Mathilde was a great collector who owned works by artists such as Tiepolo and Pontormo, a lover of *pompier* and orientalist painting, of Japanese art and of photography.

BIBLIOGRAPHY: *Un soir chez la princesse Mathilde: une Bonaparte et les arts*, exhib. cat. (Ajaccio 2019), ed. by Carole Blumenfeld *et al.* Cinisello Balsamo: Silvana, 2019.

Vanda Lisanti

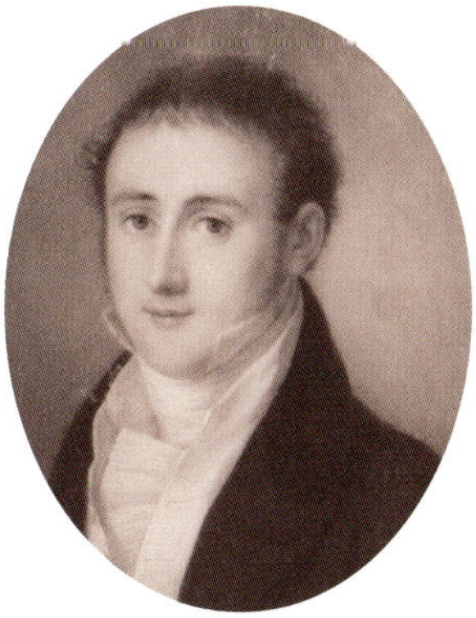

Bianca Boni

(Rome, 1786–1857)

Bianca Boni was born in Rome, in the parish of San Lorenzo in Lucina, on 6 January 1786, the daughter of the sculptor Giuseppe Boni son of Antonio, originally from Carrara, and of the Roman Anna Frangioni; she was baptized the following day with the names Blanca Aloÿsia. Her godfather was the painter from Parma Gaetano Callani (1736–1809), whom her father had met twenty years earlier at the Accademia di Belle Arti di Parma, where he had studied under Jean-Baptiste Boudard (1710–1768), a 'statuary' sculptor working for Ferdinand I, Duke of Parma. Though she probably learned the rudiments of drawing from her father, it must have been her frequentation of the studio of her Piedmontese brother-in-law Felice Festa (1763/1764–1825), a sculptor and painter of both large and miniature works, that directed Bianca's talents towards painting in watercolour and *gouache* on ivory. Indeed, Festa trained three of his four own daughters with Candida Boni as miniaturists: Giuditta Bianca Altomira called Bianca (1802–1884), Matilde Maria Giannetta (1804–1867) and Domenica Felice Virginia (1807–1881), while his oldest daughter Adelaide Felice Fortunata (1736–*post* 1845) is described as a sculptor in some parish registers between 1831 and 1836. Giuditta Bianca participated in the Paris *Salon* of 1827 with a *Portrait of a Woman* and on 4 September 1831 was elected member of the Accademia di San Luca. Domenica married the French painter Raymond Quinsac Monvoisin in Rome in 1825 and followed him to Paris in the same year. Here she worked successfully as a miniaturist and painter on porcelain, displaying her works at the *Salon* from 1831 to 1881.

On 14 February 1808, Bianca Boni married Luigi de Bustis y Figuera in the church of San Lorenzo in Lucina. She separated from him immediately afterwards for unknown reasons and never took his last name. In 1809 she participated in the exhibition held at the Capitoline with a *Blessed Virgin and Child.* On his arrival in Rome in November 1811, the French poet Alphonse de Lamartine purchased from her a *Virgin* copied from the *Madonna in Sorrow* by Guido Reni in the Galleria Corsini. As he later recalled in his *Mémoires*, during one of the sessions in which he sat for a portrait intended for his mother, Lamartine confessed to the beautiful Bianca that he had feelings for her. Bianca was so offended that she destroyed the portrait and returned the advance.

A correspondence that re-emerged only in the first half of the 20th century documents Bianca's relationship between 1814 and 1819 with a Napoleonic officer stationed in central-southern Italy, Claude-Jean (called Constant) Papillon (1778–1845). In the 1820s and 30s, she appears with regularity – with an address at Via Felice no. 30 – among the Roman artists mentioned in the guides for travellers, including the popular *Travels in Europe* by Mariana Starke. On 22 May 1825 she was elected member of the Accademia di San Luca. The last evidence of her work is an affidavit of 18 May 1844, from which it appears that she was living in Via delle Carrozze no. 98. In her will, dated 3 August 1852, she left her estate to her four artist nieces. On 27 September 1857, she died at the age of almost seventy-two, in her last home in Via della Purificazione no. 18.

BIBLIOGRAPHY: Léo R. Schidlof, *The Miniature in Europe.* 4 vols. Graz: Akademische Druck- u. Verlagsanstalt, 1964, 1:94–5; Bernardo Falconi, "Bianca Boni «miniatrice romana» (1786–1857)." *Bollettino dei musei comunali di Roma* new ser. 28 (2014), 83–110.

Alessandra Masu

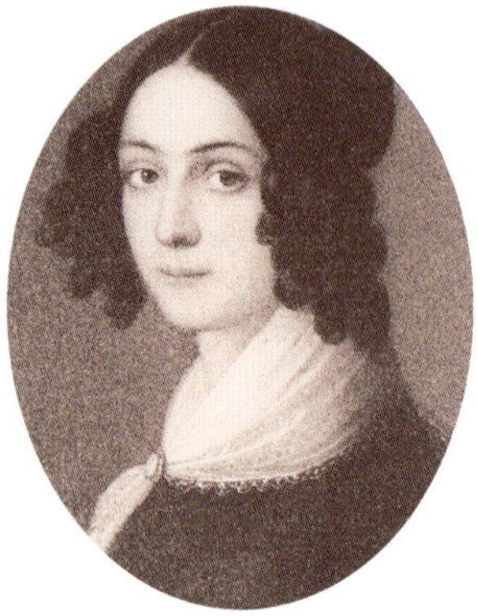

Ida Botti (Scifoni)

(Rome, 1812 – Florence, 1844)

"Idda Scifoni nata Botti romana [...]" (Idda Scifoni née Botti from Rome). This is how the painter specializing in portraits and genre painting, the daughter of Tommaso Botti and Carolina Jesi, signed herself on the back of the famous *Self-Portrait* in the Galleria d'Arte Moderna in Florence's Palazzo Pitti (inv. 1830, n. 1938). As noted by the historian Giovanni Spallicci, who included her in his "little work" devoted to "illustrious Italian women" worthy of study in schools, she began to draw at the age of nine. At fourteen she became a member of the class of painters of the Congregazione dei Virtuosi al Pantheon, having formerly been the student of Giovanni Silvagni, a well-known member of the Accademia di San Luca and, like her, of the Virtuosi al Pantheon, who had trained Amalia De Angelis and Emilia Rouillon. In 1830 Botti was living "at the Scalone di San Francesco ai Monti", as reported in the section dedicated to "History and portrait painters" of the list "for the use of foreigners" compiled and updated by Enrico de Keller. Four years later, in 1834, Giuseppe Brancadoro took up and renewed the list, giving a new address in Via del Corso no. 142. According to the testimony of Melchiorre Missirini, "she left various panels of her own composition in Rome, including "the fine story from Tasso with Erminia writing on the tree trunks the beloved name of Tancredi, purchased by Tommasini, general secretary of the Camerlengate [...] a half-length Bacchant bought by the society for the display and support of art works founded in Rome [...] Medicine, a half-length symbolic painting, kept in the home of the illustrious Roman clinician Professor Giuseppe de Mattheis". From 1836 the painter settled in Florence after mar-

Ida Botti (Scifoni), *Portrait of a Girl (Charlotte Honorine or Julie Bonaparte)*, c. 1835–39. Rome, Museo Napoleonico.

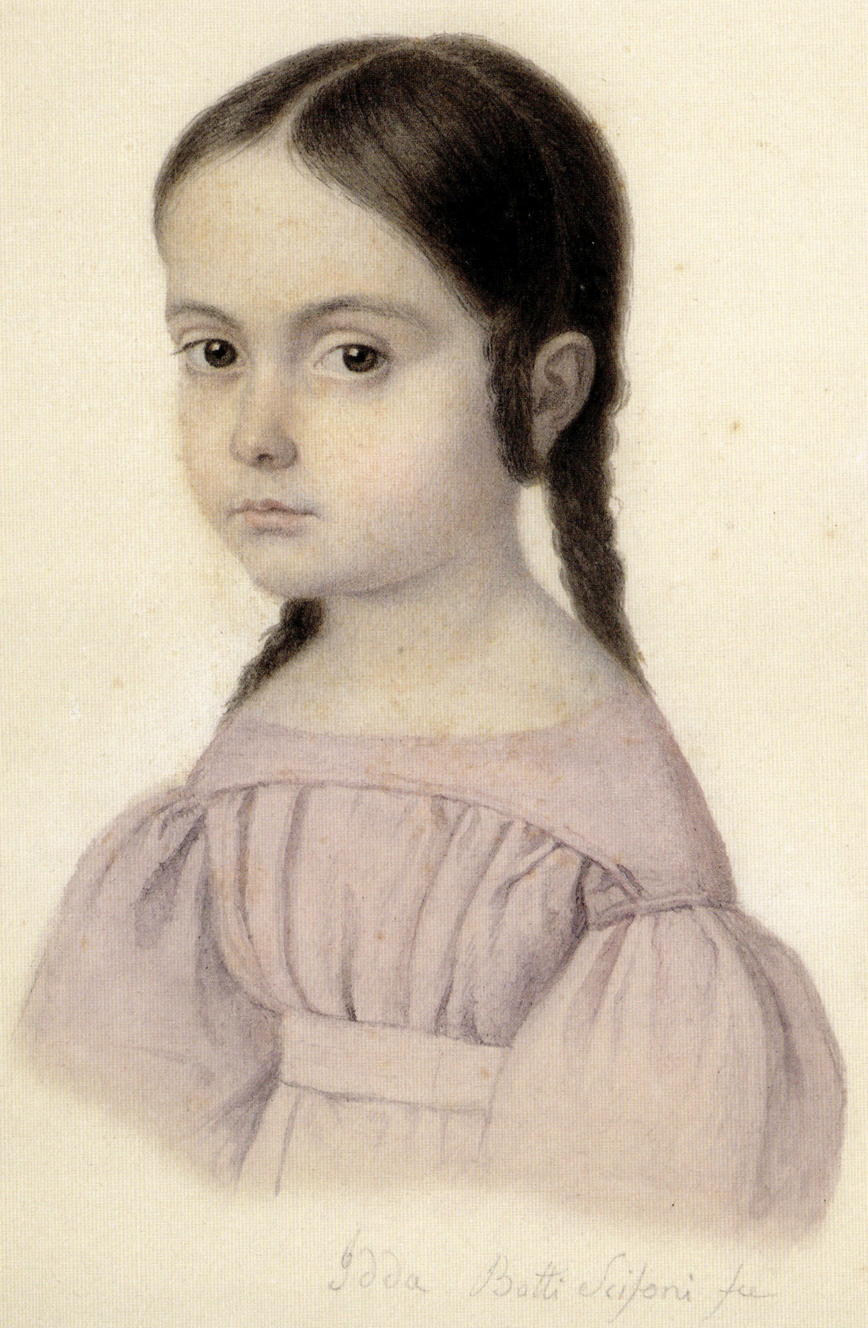
Idda Botti Scifoni fe

rying Felice Scifoni, a prominent figure in the Roman secret society of the Carbonari, who had been forced to leave the city for political reasons. Here Botti installed a small studio within Villa Demidoff, residence of the prince and collector Anatoly Demidov, where she gave painting lessons to his wife Mathilde Bonaparte, of whom she became a close friend as well as the teacher and advisor on style. She died only two years after giving birth to her only child, Anatolio Scifoni, the future painter.

BIBLIOGRAPHY: Anna Lisa Genovese, "DIARIO 1800-1834." In Vitaliano Tiberia, *La Congregazione dei Virtuosi al Pantheon da Pio VII a Pio IX*. Galatina: Congedo, 2015, 273–74.

Virginia Spadaccini

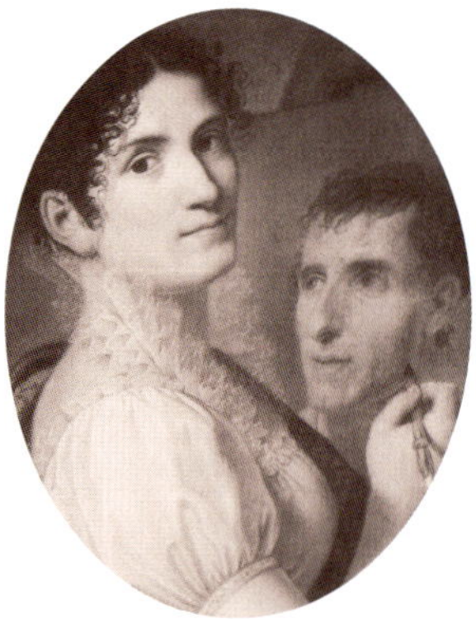

Faustina Bracci (Armellini)

(Rome, 1785–1857)

Faustina was the daughter of the architect Virginio (1738–1815) and granddaughter of the sculptor and architect Pietro Bracci (1770–1773). The earliest information on her work as a painter and copyist dates to 1806, when the Accademia di San Luca gave her permission to "move to her house the Flora by Mancini to copy it and later other paintings" (Accademia Nazionale di San Luca, Archivio Storico, *Libro delle Congregazioni*, vol. 56, fol. 63*v*), including the "Portrait of Madame Le Brun" (*ibid.*, fol. 66).

In 1810 she participated in the exhibition held in the rooms of the Palazzo del Senatore on the Capitoline, displaying two works executed in pastels: a "copy of a St Simeon" and a "Madonna after Guido Reni". In April 1811 she was elected member of the Accademia di San Luca "as a portrait painter in pastels" (*ibid.*, fol. 117*v*), on the formal proposal of the president Antonio Canova, acclaimed by the painters Gaspare Landi, Jean Baptiste Wicar and Francesco Manno.

In 1823 she became a member of the Congregazione dei Virtuosi al Pantheon together with another sixteen women painters (including Giulia Massimo Bernini, Rosa Mezzera and Marianna Candidi Dionigi) at the wishes of the director Vincenzo Martinucci and his two deputies Francesco Manno and Pietro Belli. Her obituary, published in *L'Album* on 7 March 1857, is accompanied by a short biography that describes her artistic talents: "[...] but above every art she loved painting. Using pastels with that method that Rosalba has made so famous, she gave such vigour and fulness of colour to her paintings that it was hard to discern with ease if they had been executed in oils". The epitaph carved on the monument dedicated to her in the Verano Cemetery in Rome, destroyed during the bombing of 1943, commemorated her membership of illustrious Roman institutions: "inter sodales pantheanos / bonis artibvs fovendis / et in collegivm lucanvm urbis / ob pictorivm lavdem adscitae".

BIBLIOGRAPHY: Carla Mazzarelli, "«Più vale una bella copia che un mediocre originale». Teoria e prassi e mercato della copia a Roma fra Sette e Ottocento." In *Promuovere le arti. Intermediari, pubblico e mercato a Roma fra XVIII e XIX secolo*, ed. by Serenella Rolfi Ožvald. Rome: Carocci, 2006, 27; E. Camboni, in *Canova. Eterna bellezza*, exhib. cat. (Rome 2019–20), ed. by Giuseppe Pavanello. Cinisello Balsamo: Silvana, 2019, 284.

Michela D'Agostino

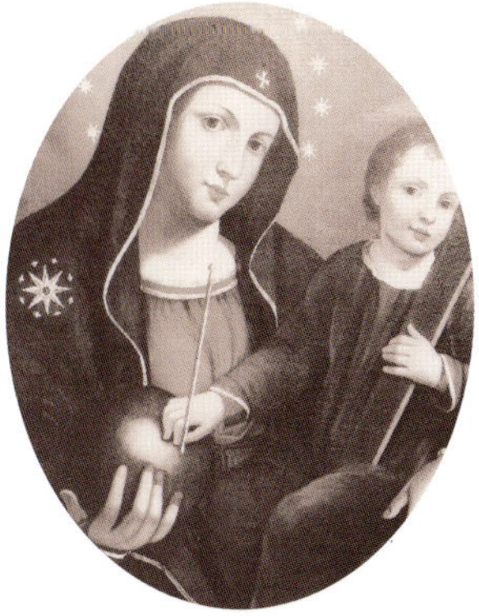

Plautilla Bricci

(Rome, 1616–1692)

A multi-talented artist, famed as a draughtswoman, painter and architect, Plautilla Bricci was the daughter of the actor, musician and painter Giovanni (1579–1645), a student of the Cavalier d'Arpino. In her father's workshop she learned the first rudiments of drawing and painting, and acquired a remarkable creative versatility. Her first public work was the image of the Virgin of Carmel executed for the Carmelite friars of Monte Santo, destined for a chapel that no longer exists and now on the high altar of the church of Santa Maria in Montesanto in Piazza del Popolo. Her close connection to the Carmelite friars probably allowed her access to the convent of San Giuseppe a Capo Le Case, where she met Flavia Benedetti (1597–1676), an oblate with the name of Maria Eufrasia della Croce and sister of the Abbot Elpidio (1609–1690). Her fruitful collaboration with Prior Benedetti put her in contact with Cardinal Jules Mazarin, for whom she made two drawings for his funerary monument in 1657 and, in 1660, two designs based on ideas by Benedetti for the Spanish steps at Trinità dei Monti (Biblioteca Apostolica Vaticana, Chigi P. VII 10, pt. B, fols 30-31; Stockholm, Nationalmuseum, inv. NMH CC 790). In 1655, a document held at the Accademia di San Luca lists her among the members of the academy together with her brother, the painter Basilio (1621–1692), for the gift of "two *testone* coins" in silver.

Dating to 1663 are the seven drawings (now in the Archivio di Stato di Roma) executed by "the architect Plautilla Briccia, elected member in this capacity" for Villa Benedetti at San Pancrazio. The suburban residence of Elpidio Benedetti was "constructed in the form of a ship on a rock" and suffered severe damage during the siege of Rome in 1849. Between 1662 and 1675, she was entrusted with two commissions for the Lateran worksite: the lunette depicting the *Presentation of the Sacred Heart of Jesus to the Eternal Father* (now in the storerooms of the Vatican Museums), executed between 1669 and 1675, and the two lost canvases with Sts Francis and Dominic for the oratory of the Santissimo Sacramento, commissioned by the priest Giovanni Fortunato between 1662 and 1670. Additionally, between 1676 and 1678, in collaboration with her brother Basilio, Plautilla supplied the clay models for the ornaments, reliefs and two flying angels for the reliquary cabinet to be placed on the top of the church's ciborium. In her dual capacity as painter and architect she designed, on commission from Elpidio Benedetti, the chapel of St Louis IX in the church of San Luigi dei Francesi and the altarpiece with *St Louis IX of France Between History and Faith.*

In November 1692, Plautilla died at the age of seventy-six at her house "located in Trastevere near San Francesco a Ripa", bequeathed to her by Abbot Benedetti.

Bibliography: Melania Mazzucco, *L'architettrice.* Torino: Einaudi, 2021; *Una rivoluzione silenziosa: Plautilla Bricci, pittrice e architettrice*, exhib. cat. (Rome 2021–22), ed. by Yuri Primarosa. Rome: Officina Libraria, 2021.

Michela D'Agostino

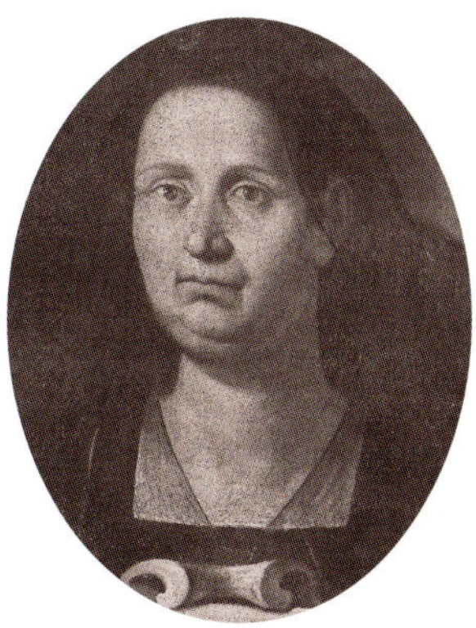

Girolama Cagnucci (Parasole)

(?, c. 1567 – Rome, 1622)

Girolama Cagnucci (the reading of her last name found in period documents, preferable to Cagnaccia, used in some printed sources and still prevalent in the art-historical literature) was an artist

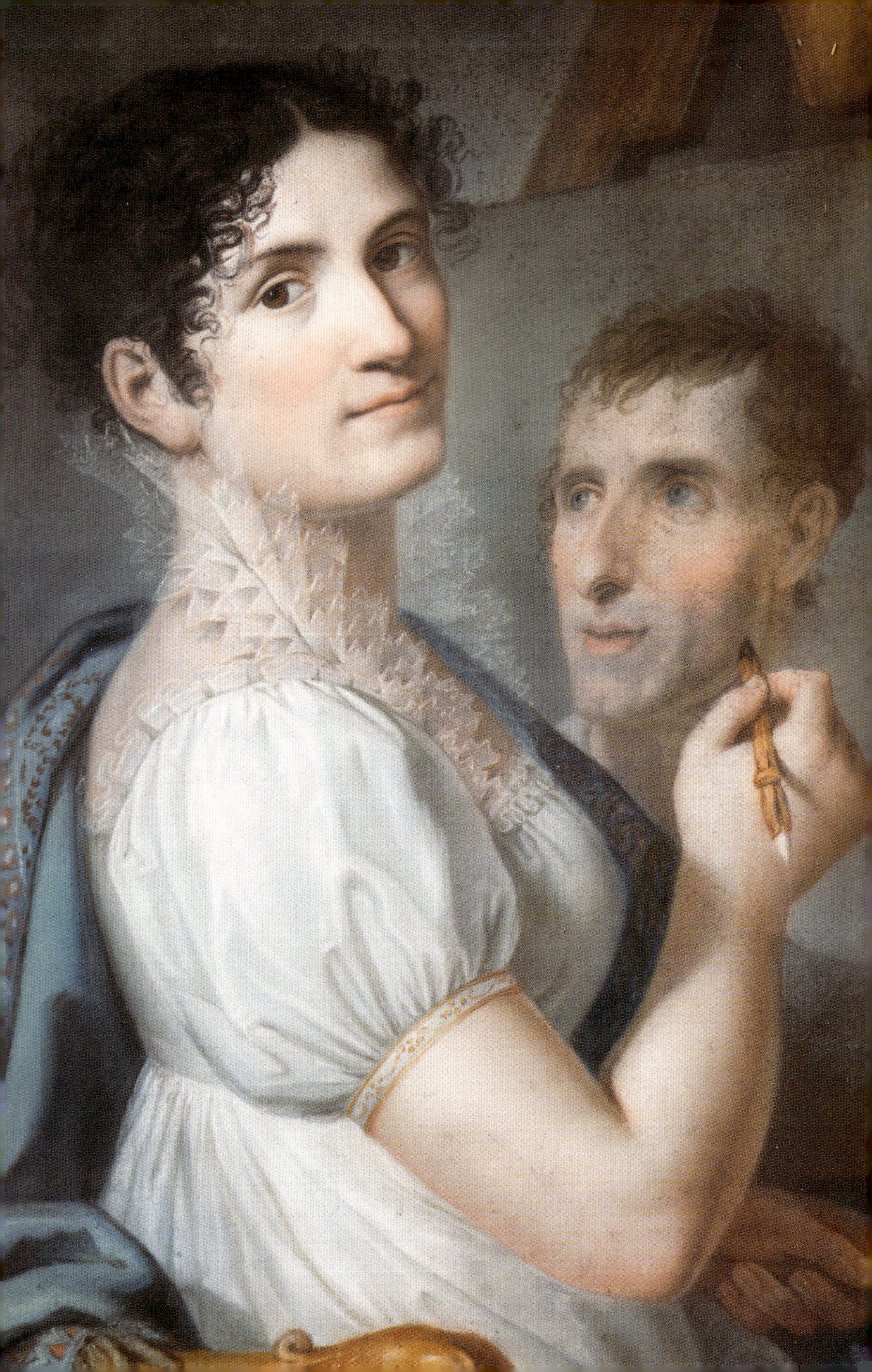

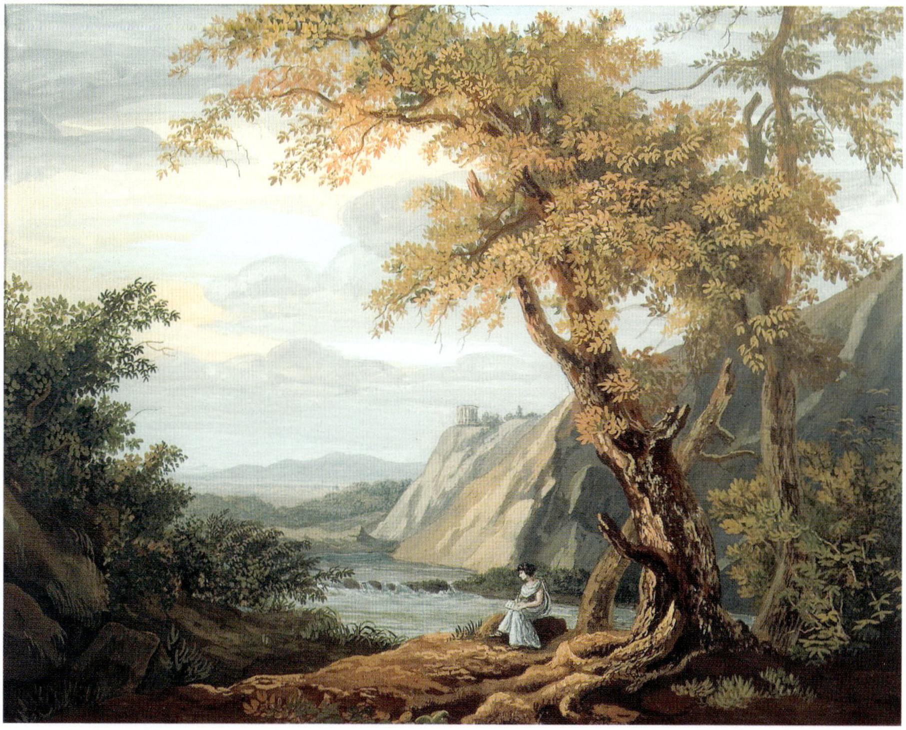

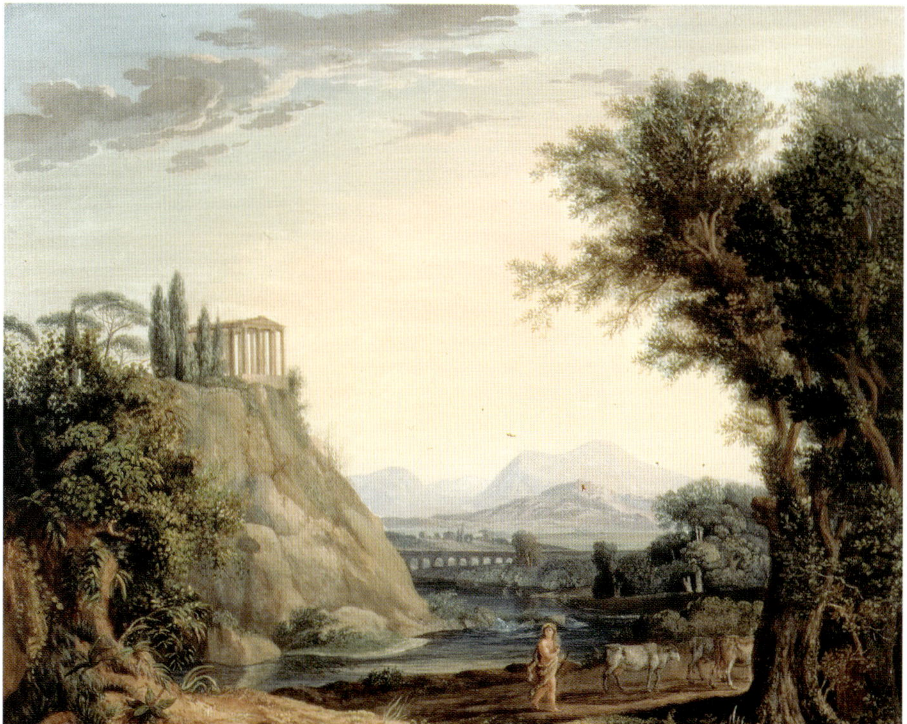

Faustina Bracci (Armellini), *Self-Portrait*, 1811. Rome, Accademia Nazionale di San Luca.

Marianna Candidi (Dionigi), *The Aniene in Tivoli* and *Landscape with Hercules Leading the Cattle of Geryon*, c. 1798. Rome, Galleria Nazionale d'Arte Moderna e Contemporanea.

specializing in woodcut engraving. She worked in this genre partly in collaboration with her husband Leonardo Parasole, himself a woodcut artist and publisher at the head of a prolific family workshop. Their son Bernardino (1594–*post* 1624) was a painter and student of the Cavalier d'Arpino. Due to an oversight, Giovanni Baglione named a non-existent Isabella as Leonardo's wife, fusing into a single brief biographical profile information referring to Girolama and facts relating to her sister-in-law Elisabetta Cattaneo; this mistake, clarified only recently (Pupillo 2009), conditioned the subsequent literature on the woodcut artist. Documentary sources, too, are scanty, making the reconstruction of her artistic career difficult and sometimes incomplete. With Leonardo she executed the illustrations for some printed books in the early 1590s, signing herself with her monogram ("GaPï" or variants) accompanied by the drawing of a stylus. Her most important and complex work was the large woodcut with the *Battle of the Centaurs and Lapiths*, after a drawing by Antonio Tempesta (Chicago, The Art Institute, inv. 1999.684). Other prints by Girolama are listed in the biographical entry authored by Maria Rosaria Mancino published in the *Dizionario biografico degli Italiani* (2015); of them, those initialled "PM" or "PMF" should be expunged as they have been shown to be the work of Paul Maupin. The "engravings in the book of plants of Prince Cesi" mentioned by Giovanni Baglione should likely be identified as the botanical illustrations of the *Mexicanarum plantarum imagines* (1613; BAV, Stamp. barb. N.VI.175). It is probable that the artist was a member of the Accademia di San Luca (though there are no documents to prove this), which possesses an oil portrait depicting her in widow's weeds. Girolama Cagnucci died at the age of 55 in Rome on 8 July 1622 in the parish of Santi Vincenzo e Anastasio a Trevi and was buried in the Oratorian church of Santa Maria in Vallicella, whose spiritual teachings both she and her husband adhered to. The parish record of her death describes her as a "sculptor and painter".

BIBLIOGRAPHY: Marco Pupillo, "Gli incisori di Baronio. Il maestro «MGF», Philippe Thomassin, Leonardo e Girolama Parasole (con una nota su Isabella/Isabetta/Elisabetta Parasole)." In *Baronio e le sue fonti*, ed. by Luigi Gulia. Sora: Centro Studi Vincenzo Patriarca, 2009, 845–50; Evelyn Lincoln, "The Parasole Family Enterprise and Book Illustration at the Medici Press." In *The Medici Oriental Press: Knowledge and Cultural Transfer around 1600*, ed. by Eckhard Leuschner, Gerhard Wolf. Florence: Olschki, 2022, 111–15.

Marco Pupillo

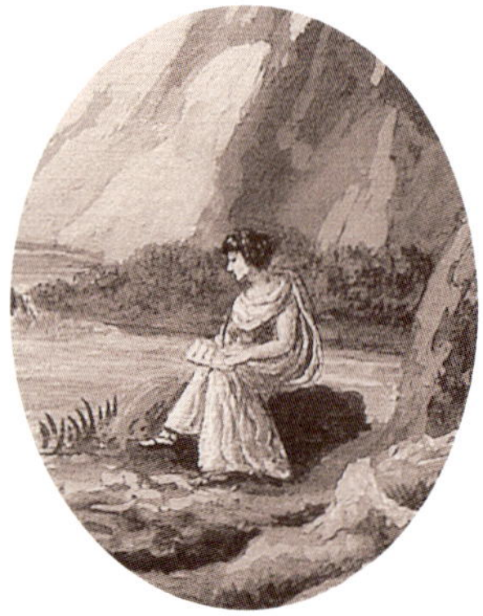

Marianna Candidi (Dionigi)

(Rome, 1756 – Lanuvio, 1826)

The daughter of the doctor Giuseppe Candidi and of Maddalena Scilla (a descendant of the Sicilian painter Agostino), Marianna Candidi was a painter, musician and scholar of languages, archaeology and classics active between the 18th and 19th centuries. Her salon in Palazzo Verospi Vitelleschi in Rome was frequented by the most important cultural figures of the time. Widely respected, she was invited before the Revolution to the French court to act as governess to one of the princesses, an offer that she declined as she did not wish to leave her children and husband (the Ferrarese nobleman Domenico Dionigi, whom she had married when she was fifteen). A student of Carlo Labruzzi, as an artist she was essentially a landscape painter, a genre that was developing a new and specific identity during her lifetime, arriving at its first theoretical codifications. Marianna contributed to these with a treatise entitled *Precetti elementari sulla pittura de' paesi*, published by the De Romanis printshop in 1816. However, her most famous work is the *Viaggi in alcune città del Lazio che diconsi fondate dal re Saturno* of 1809, a pioneering collection of prints devoted to the theme of the megalithic walls of towns in the Lazio region.

The first woman archaeologist, Marianna died in her seventies and was a member of numerous Roman, Italian and foreign academies (Charlestown,

South Carolina). Her funerary oration composed by the antiquary Luigi Cardinali, published in the *Memorie romane di antichità e di belle arti* of 1826, contains a list of her paintings. The heading "My Landscapes" suggests that the mythological or historical subjects mentioned here (*Horace Among the Lucretili Mountains, The Infant Moses on the Nile, Mars and Rhea Silvia by the Tiber* are just some of the titles) were 'historiated' landscapes, a format in vogue in Rome at the time. Of her seven children, the cultural tradition of the family was continued by Carolina (whose dates of birth and death are unknown but who in 1796 was already the wife of Pietro Stampa, whom she married as an adolescent) and Enrichetta (1784–1868), also a painter and member of the Arcadian Academy, often remembered among the correspondents of Giacomo Leopardi.

BIBLIOGRAPHY: *Marianna Candidi Dionigi paesaggista e viaggiatrice*, conference proceedings (Rome 2011), ed. by Vincenzo De Caprio. Rome: Viella, 2014.

Tiziano Casola

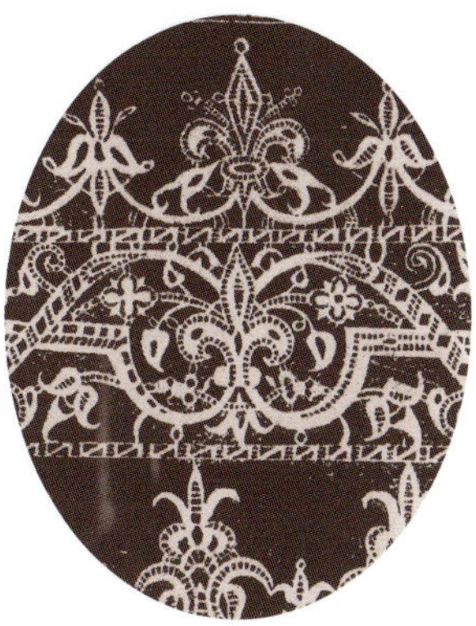

Elisabetta (or Isabetta) Cattaneo (Parasole)

(Bergamo?, *c.* 1578 – Rome, 1617)

Elisabetta (or Isabetta, in both documents and printed works), daughter of 'Baron Cattaneo of Bergamo' and of Faustina, grew up in Rome in the convent school of Santa Caterina della Rosa for reasons that remain unclear. This institution hosted daughters of members of the Curia as well as girls who had been orphaned or came from poor families and were at risk of being trafficked into the sex trade. They were provided with dowries by the archconfraternity and educated by the Augustinian nuns in 'domestic arts' like embroidery and sewing. In 1593 she married Rosato Parasole, a mosaicist working at the Vatican Mosaic Studio. He introduced her into the family workshop, headed by his brother Leonardo, a woodcut printer and publisher. In this new environment, her talent for inventing new forms of embroidery became an entrepreneurial activity in its own right. In 1595, signing herself "Isabetta Catanea Parasole", she published the *Specchio delle virtuose donne* "at the request" of Rosato. This was a collection of 37 rectangular woodcut plates with illustrations showing pieces of lace to be made using a variety of techniques, preceded by a dedication to the Duchess of Sermoneta. The work was so successful that it was reprinted twice (in 1596 and 1598). In 1597 she published a new collection, the *Studio delle virtuose dame*, with a double dedication – in Spanish and Italian – to "Donna Giovanna D'Aragona, et Cardona". In the following years she continued to publish a very popular series of pattern books aimed at a female audience all adopting the same format without a commentary on the plates. Elisabetta is named as the author of the drawings and it is possible that the woodcuts, which are not signed, were carved by other members of the family business. In his *Life* dedicated to the Parasole family, Giovanni Baglione attributes the volume to Isabella, a name given to the author only twice: in the Spanish dedication of the *Studio*, a printing error for the more unusual Isabetta, and in the *Pretiosa gemma*, published in Venice, due to an oversight by the editor. Giovanni Baglione says that Isabella was the wife of Leonardo Parasole and also ascribed to her some botanical illustrations, which should probably be attributed to her sister-in-law Girolama Cagnucci. This error, emended only a few years ago, has conditioned all of the subsequent literature. There is currently no evidence that Elisabetta was responsible for works other than the pattern books mentioned above. She died in Rome on 12 May 1617. The documents often give her birthplace as Bergamo; only on the title page of her final work is she described as Roman.

BIBLIOGRAPHY: *see* Girolama Cagnucci (Parasole).

Marco Pupillo

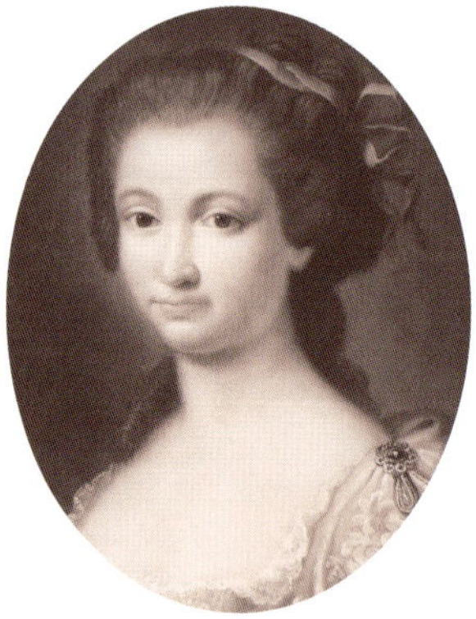

Caterina Cherubini (Preciado)

(Rome, *c.* 1728–1811)

Caterina Cherubini's work is mentioned by numerous sources, none of which predates 1750, the year of her marriage to the Spanish artist Francisco Preciado de La Vega (1712–1789), from 1758 supervisor of the Spanish artists who had won bursaries to study in Rome. By this time the painter, thought to belong to a family originally from Aragon and, as clarified by the studies, no relation to the painter Giovanni Domenico Cherubini, had already received an artistic education in her husband's studio. After specializing in copying the masterpieces belonging to Roman collections, Caterina embarked upon a highly productive and much appreciated career as a miniaturist. Thanks to this work, she was proposed by the Spanish ambassador Manuel de Roda y Arrieta as a candidate for the position of *Chamber Painter* to the king of Spain, "a rash judgement: I am not enamoured of her, as the faces that she paints are more beautiful than her own". This testimony refers to her earliest known works, like the faces modelled on Carlo Maratti, including that donated in 1760 to the Accademia di San Luca when she was elected member (inv. 497) and the *Madonna and Child* presented in 1763 to the monastery of the Santissima Trinità degli Spagnoli. The painting in oil on canvas depicting *Justice and Peace*, a copy after Ciro Ferri, is connected to her appointment to the Real Academia de Bellas Artes de San Fernando in Madrid in 1761 (inv. 0208), while a copy after Guercino that has not been traced marks her election to the Accademia Clementina in Bologna (1778). Caterina Cherubini is also known to have had an interest in literary writing that dates to over ten years earlier; already in 1766, she had become a member of the Arcadian Academy with the pseudonym of Ersilla Ateneia. The works mentioned in the documents are very numerous: the *St Francis Consoled by the Angel* (Valladolid, private collection) dates to 1769, as does the exquisite little painting of *St Agnes* in the Museo del Prado (inv. P004699). Her most important set of works is the series of miniatures sent from Rome to Madrid at annual intervals from 1774 to 1804, fulfilling the obligation incurred when the King of Spain Carlos III granted the painter 3000 *reales*. None of these copies, mentioned in the correspondence between José Nicolas de Azara, José Moñino y Redondo Count of Floridablanca and Marquis Girolamo Grimaldi, can be traced. However, it is credible that within the royal collections they formed a *cabinet de réception* by one of the most talented European miniaturists, as can be seen today in a watercolour after Guido Reni's *Dawn* (Tarragona, Martínez Lanzas collection). A self-portrait by the painter was in the collection of the Marquises of Loreto in Seville, while a portrait of her traditionally attributed to Anton von Maron is in the Accademia di San Luca (inv. 450).

BIBLIOGRAPHY: Jesús Urrea, *Relaciones artísticas hispano-romanas en el siglo XVIII*. Madrid: Fundación de Apoyo a la Historia del Arte Hispánico, 2006, 161–65.

Vanda Lisanti

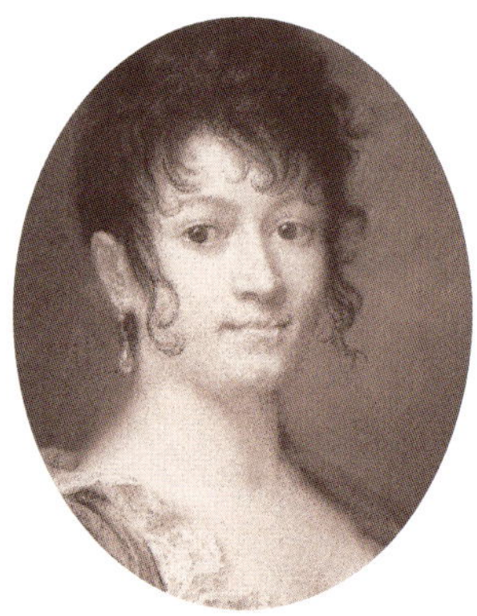

Sofia Clerk (Giordano)

(Turin, 1778–1829)

Sofia Clerk was born in Turin on 30 April 1778. Perhaps the daughter of the painter Pietro Antonio Clerk, she began to study painting from childhood on the advice of the printmaker and draughtsman Pietro Giacomo Palmieri, who recognized her precocious talent. Thanks to the financial support of

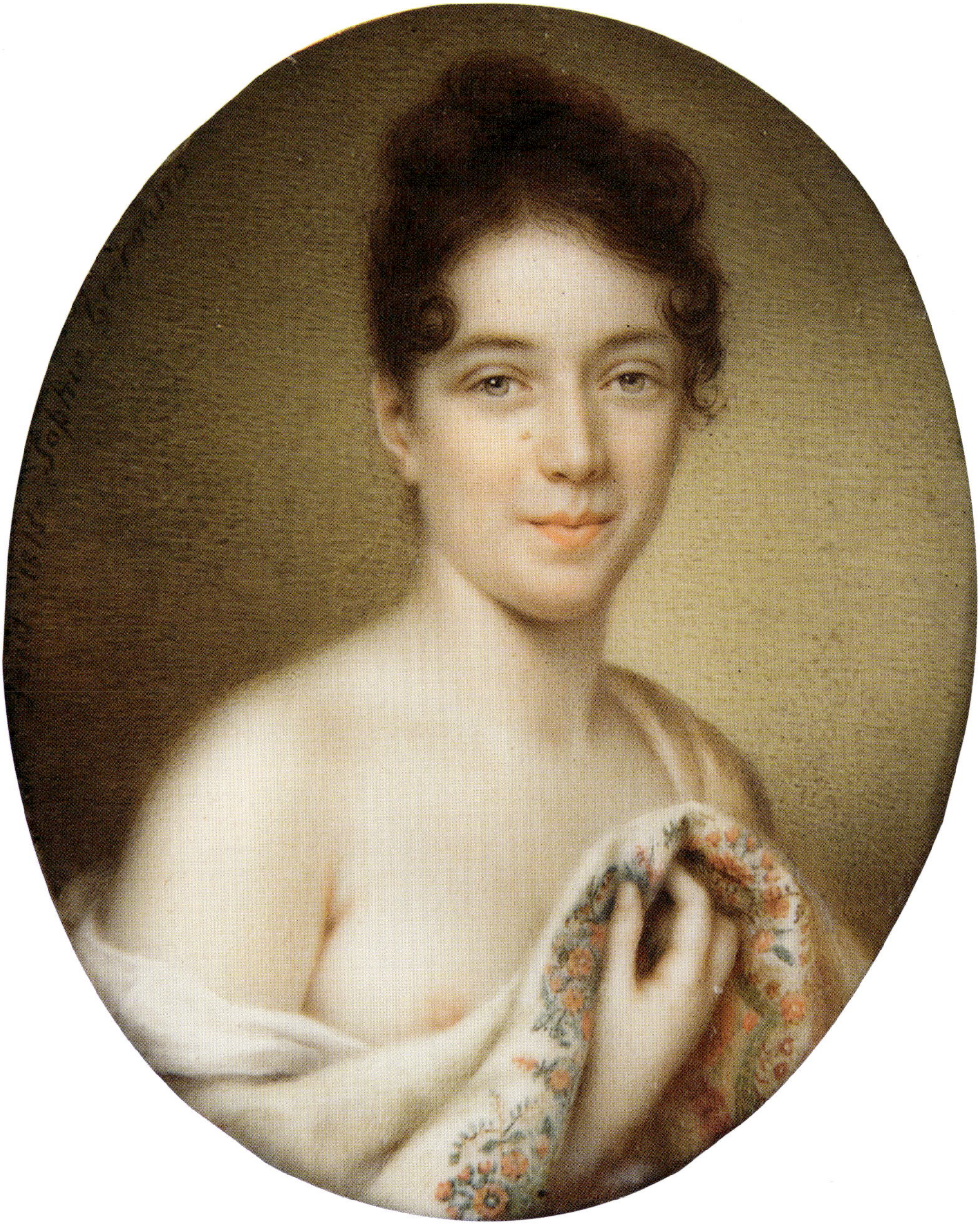

Sofia Clerk (Giordano), *Portrait of a Young Woman*, 1815. Turin, Musei Reali, Galleria Sabauda.

Giacinto Vinay, counsellor of the prefecture and her guardian and patron, she was able to travel to Rome at the age of eighteen to take lessons from Therese Concordia Mengs. The young pupil's artistic education thus took place in the studio of this well-known miniaturist, who specialized in pastels and enamel painting. Under the guidance of Therese Mengs, sister of the famous Neoclassical painter Anton Raphael Mengs and wife of the Austrian portraitist Anton von Maron, and in contact with the cosmopolitan environment of the papal city, Sofia practiced by copying the old masters and making life drawings, devoting herself to the execution of pastel portraits and miniature copies of paintings by important artists of the 16th and 17th centuries.

On 17 September 1801, she was elected "member, as a figure painter in miniature and in pastels" (letter from Andrea Vici to Sofia Clerk) of the Roman Accademia di San Luca, which owns a portrait of her executed for the occasion by Giovanni Domenico Cherubini. On her appointment, a miniature depicting *Innocence*, whose whereabouts are now unknown, was selected among the works presented by the artist as a permanent gift to the Accademia.

When she returned to the Savoy capital towards the end of the same year, she continued her work as a painter, executing both pastel works and miniatures on ivory or parchment. On 19 December 1802 she received her appointment to "corresponding member of the department of literature and arts" (letter from Francesco Regis to Sofia Clerk) from the members of the Accademia delle Scienze in Turin.

Her marriage to the doctor Giovanni Domenico Maria Giordano dates to 1803; the couple had two sons, Scipione and Emilio.

Between 1805 and 1829, the artist participated on several occasions in the Turin *Salons*, presenting miniatures and pastels. Most of these depicted works by the classicist Bolognese painters of the 17th century or portraits of illustrious Piedmontese cultural figures, earning her the unanimous respect of her colleagues and of the public. At the first exhibition held in April 1805, on the occasion of Napoleone Bonaparte's visit to Turin, the artist displayed four works drawn from canvases by Guido Reni and Francesco Albani. These may have been painted during her time in Rome, as perhaps confirmed by the valuation "of the eight miniatures executed in Rome after the large original paintings by the famous Sofia Giordano" drawn up at the request of the painter's husband on 25 July 1844 by Pietro Giovanni Palmieri, son of the engraver Pietro Giacomo.

On 25 August 1812, Sofia Clerk was awarded the gold medal for the works displayed at the Academy's exhibition, held annually on 15 August, by Prospero Balbo, rector of the Accademia delle Scienze of Turin and inspector general of the Imperial University.

The painter died in Turin on 26 April 1829. Her obituary, published in the *Gazzetta piemontese* on 14 May, celebrates her talent, her ability to interpret the creations of the great masters of the past "preserving the character of the technique of each artist, the colouring, the chiaroscuro, and the expressions of each figure" and her ability in her portraits "to reveal [...] the spirit of the person". It also recalls "the precious collection of paintings" present on her death in the family home, including her *Self-Portrait* and the portraits on parchment of Therese Mengs and Anton von Maron (Turin, Musei Reali, Galleria Sabauda, inv. 697, 715).

BIBLIOGRAPHY: Barbara Stabielli, "«La femminea virtù pittorica». La figura di Sofia Giordano Clerc." *Bollettino della Società Piemontese di Archeologia e Belle Arti* new ser. 49-50 (2008–9), 165–87.; Neil Jeffares, s.v. "Giordano, sig.ra Giovanni, née Sofia Clerc." In *Dictionary of Pastellists Before 1800*, ed. online 2008, last update: February 27, 2018.

Sofia Villano

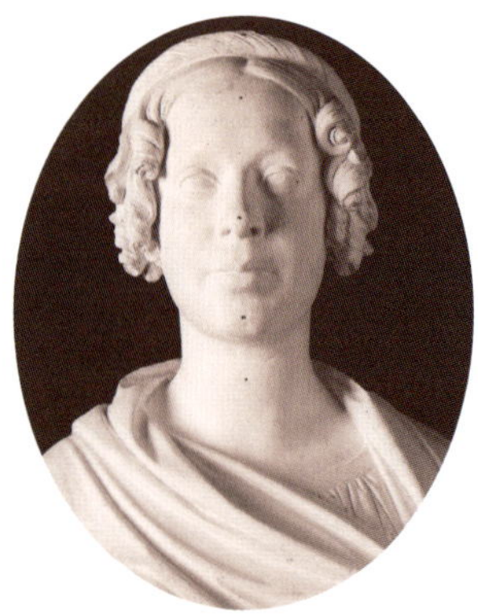

Chiara Colonna

(Rome, 1793–1847)

Chiara Colonna, a Roman noblewoman from a very prominent family, the daughter of Don Fabrizio Colonna and of Bianca Doria del Carretto, is known above all as a draughtswoman working under the guidance of Tommaso Minardi (Faenza, 1787 – Rome, 1871). As attested by the correspondence preserved in the Ovidi Fonds of the Archivio di Stato di Roma, which represents the documentary corpus of reference for reconstructing Colonna's apprenticeship, her initial contacts with her teacher, friend and protégé from Faenza date to 1830. The letters written by the noblewoman reveal her dedication to the practice of art, inside and outside the palace walls. In the 1830s, Colonna visited various cities in Italy. In Florence, Bologna and Urbino, faithful to the teachings of Minardi, who often accompanied her on her travels, she studied the old masters. Her interest in early art is the most obvious stylistic feature of Colonna's tiny oeuvre, consisting of a very few drawings: the lunette with the *Madonna and Child With the Young Baptist* (Rome, private collection), another variation on the same subject (1835, della Porta collection) – both probably based on inventions by Minardi – and the album recently discovered in Palazzo Colonna. The latter contains sixty drawings that can be dated to between the third and final decade of the 19th century, of which over a third are signed by Chiara Colonna or attributed to her.

A profoundly cultured woman, also well-versed in poetry and music, Colonna was a lively participant in the artistic, cultural and political life of Restoration Rome. Thanks to her prestige, she exerted a degree of influence: she provided subsidies to artists, developed ties with intellectuals and men of power, even lobbying for elections to cardinal, like that of the future Pope Giovanni Maria Mastai Ferretti, who found in Chiara Colonna one of his most fervent supporters.

BIBLIOGRAPHY: Fernando Mazzocca, Ilaria Pallavicino Miani, in *Le Bateau de récréation. Album romantico 1820-1830*, exhib. cat. (Rome 1983–84), ed. by Fernando Mazzocca. Rome: Galleria Carlo Virgilio, 1983, 34–5, no. 7; Stefano Susinno, "Nobili dilettanti a scuola dal Minardi." In *Il salotto delle caricature. Acquerelli di Filippo Caetani 1830-1860*, exhib. cat. (Rome 1999), ed. by Giulia Gorgone, Cristina Cannelli. Rome: L'Erma di Bretschneider, 1999, 39–40.

Jessica Calipari

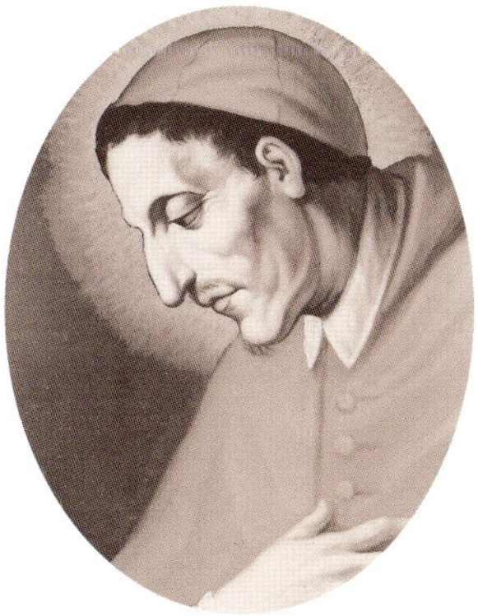

Faustina Concioli

(Rome, 1780 – Gaeta, known until 1821)

Faustina Concioli, "a good draughtswoman and a charming painter", was born in Rome in 1780. Her father was Antonio Concioli (1739–1820), a well-known painter and probably the only direct student of Pompeo Batoni; already from an early age she had thus been able to study in his workshop. In Rome she became known as a painter, executing the *Portrait of Cardinal Giuseppe Maria Tommasi* in 1804 (Rome, Museo di Roma, Dep. Arc. 25). In 1806, her first public commission, for the monumental altarpiece for the church of Santa Maria di Loreto depicting the *Madonna Enthroned with the Child and Sts Antony, Catherine and Onuphrius* (now in the sacristy), earned her the plaudits of the *Diario ordinario.* The newspaper predicted that this "talented young woman will certainly turn out to be an excellent painter; the public hopes that from her brush will come works of even greater taste and perfection in the future". The hopes of the Roman press were partially disappointed when, after marrying Francesco Antonio Notarianni, a famous naturalist and botanist, on 26 December 1808, the couple moved to Gaeta in 1809 following the Napoleonic occupation. There Faustina became the mother of two daughters and added musical and literary activities to the practice of painting, as jokingly recalled in a song dedicated to her by Count Trojano Marulli in 1816 ("You play and sing marvellously / you write verses better than Martelli / you paint, and your style resembles Guido"). The painter's personality is also reflected in the list of items making up her dowry, chief among them a harpsichord. While this document is certainly evidence of the wealth and fame attained by her father Antonio in Rome (Verdirosi 2015), it is equally important to stress that when it was signed Faustina was twenty-eight and had already been painting for some time. As such, we cannot rule out that some of the paintings listed in the dowry agreement, as well as being originals as mentioned in the document, were by her own hand.

BIBLIOGRAPHY: Roberto Verdirosi, "Per un profilo di Antonio Concioli: pittore della bottega di Pompeo Batoni." *Studi di storia dell'arte* 26 (2015), 237, 246, 253–54, 263–64.

Vanda Lisanti

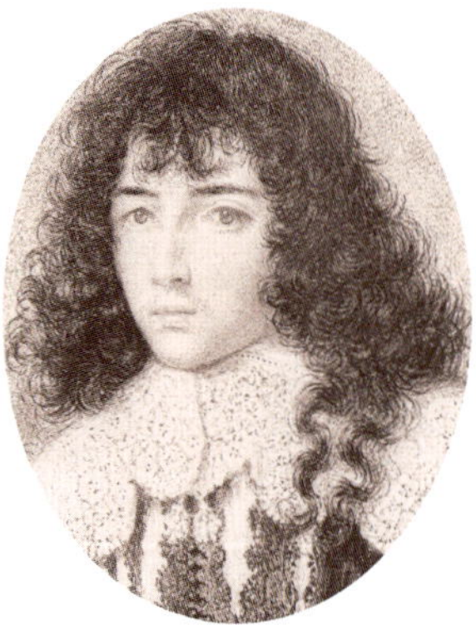

Maddalena Corvini

(Rome, 1607–1664)

Born on 17 October 1607, Maddalena Corvini grew up in a stimulating environment. Her father, Enrico Corvino, had been a well-known pharmacist in Delft, and her mother, Caterina Castelli, was the daughter of the Belgian miniaturist Frans van de Casteele, documented in Rome from 1577. Maddalena thus learned the art of miniature painting from her grandfather and her uncle Michele (1587–1636), miniaturist in turn mentioned by Giovanni Baglione, while her apprenticeship with Guido Reni, mentioned only in the primogeniture inventory of the Ruffo collection (1710), remains in doubt. At the end of the 1630s her renown is attested by the inclusion of her portrait (1636, preparatory drawing in Frankfurt, Stadelsches Kunstinstitut, inv. 1025) in a series of drawings and prints with portraits of women painters executed by Claude Mellan between 1626 and 1636. She was also supported and advanced in her professional career by Cassiano dal Pozzo, a family friend, as suggested by his role as executor of her mother's will. Though there is no evidence of Maddalena's participation in the *Museum cartaceum*, it is likely that she was involved thanks to Cassiano himself, highly appreciative of her talents as a miniaturist as is evident from a letter of 1659 from Carlo Maria dal Pozzo to Carlo Dati. A further achievement was her involvement in some papal commissions with the execution of various miniatures, including a page of the *Benedictional* of Urban VIII, now in Toledo (Biblioteca Capitular, ms. 38.12). Among her known works, the *Madonna and Child* (Florence, Galleria Palatina, inv. 5574) bears the inscription "Rome 1640". Other miniatures have appeared on the art market: particularly interesting among these is a *St Catherine of Alexandria* (Norfolk, private collection) maybe a portrait of Artemisia Gentileschi (recently displayed at the exhibition *Maestras. Women Masters 1500–1900* at the Arp Museum in Remagen). The artist was thus clearly well integrated into the art world, as confirmed by her presence among the members of the Accademia di San Luca in 1655. Also plausible is the report by Filippo Baldinucci according to which Anna Angelica Allegrini (Rome, 1631?–1686), daughter of Flaminio Allegrini from Gubbio, was her student, though hitherto no work has been attributed to her. Equally significant is the testimony of Abraham Brueghel, who lamented her demise in 1666, just a few years after her death (1664), telling Antonio Ruffo that of the artist's miniatures "his brother had a few little pieces, but thought a great deal of them". The fact that his brother owned some of her small format works is also confirmed by Giovanni Pietro Bellori in his brief description of Corvini's "Museum of natural things and of various ancient and foreign curiosities".

BIBLIOGRAPHY: *Codici della Cappella Sistina: manoscritti miniati in collezioni spagnole (CEEH Centro de Estudios Europa Hispánica)*, ed. by Elena De Laurentiis, Emilia Anna Talamo. Rome: Campisano, 2010, 42–5, 66–7, 277.

Ilaria Arcangeli

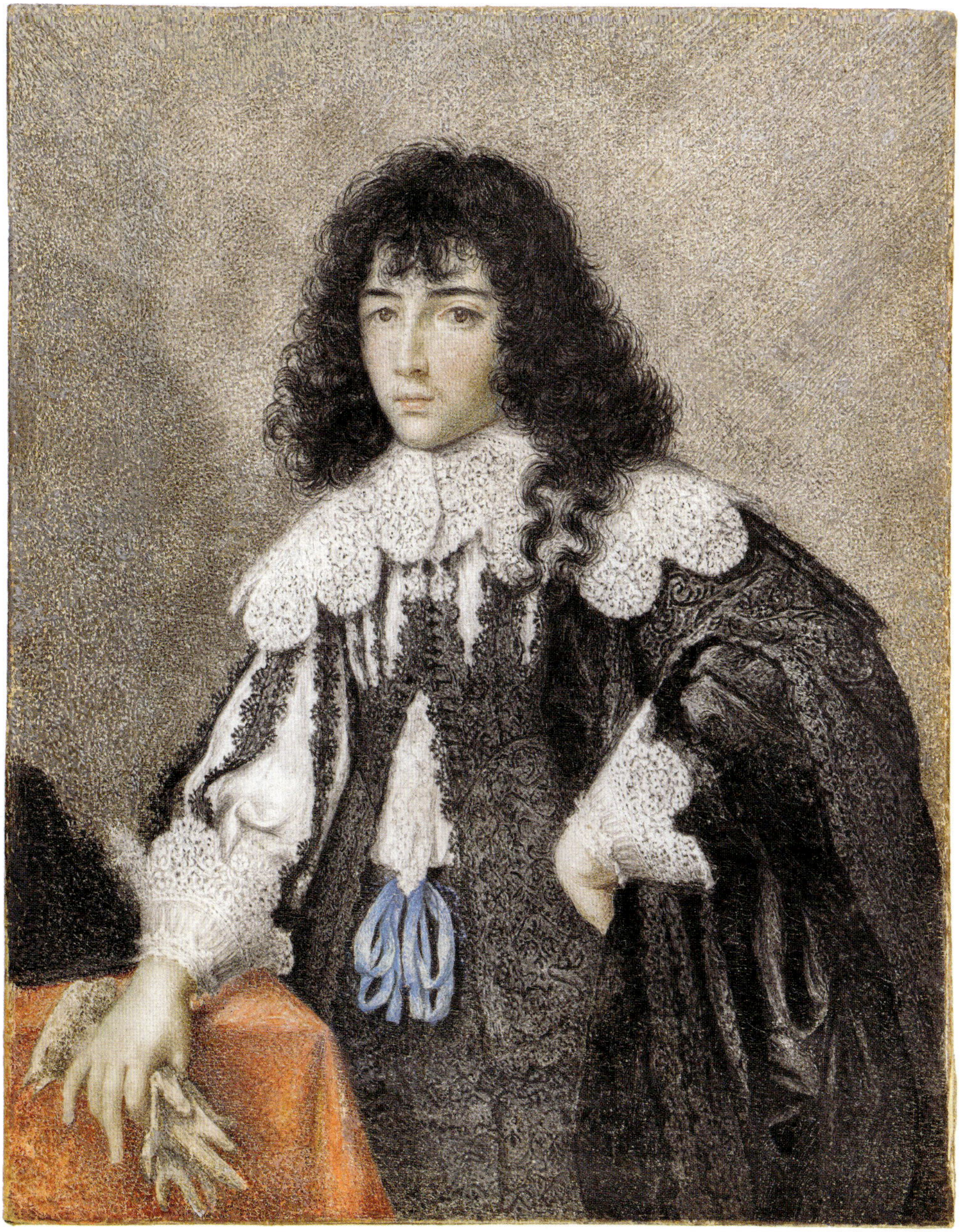

Maddalena Corvini, *Young Man with Gloves*, 1639. Ferrara, Fondazione Cavallini-Sgarbi.

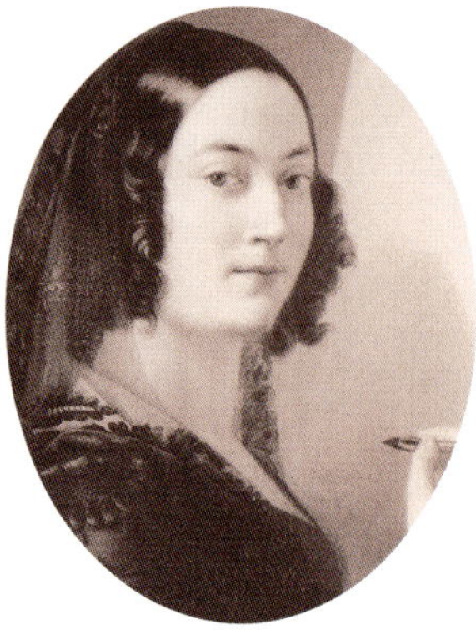

Amalia De Angelis (Salducci)

(Rome, 1824–1873)

The daughter of Nicola De Angelis, a professor of veterinary science at the University of Rome, and of Anna Silvagni, Amalia was soon entrusted to the teachings of Giovanni Silvagni, having shown an inclination towards art since childhood.

It was probably the painter who opened the doors for her to become a member of the Congregazione dei Virtuosi al Pantheon at the age of only thirteen, in defiance of the rules set down in its statutes which specified a minimum age of twenty-five. Her appointment is confirmed by a letter sent to the society on 12 August 1837, in which she thanks them for the honour accorded her.

In 1844, De Angelis was awarded a special prize at the Clementino-Pellegrini competition held by the Accademia di San Luca, praised both for a painting depicting the Lord at the temple in the act of pronouncing the phrase: "Render therefore unto Caesar the things which are Caesar's, and unto God the things that are God's", and for her daring as the first woman to participate.

The following year, she won the third Gregoriano competition, established by the society of the Virtuosi al Pantheon, with the work *St Lawrence Presents the Treasures of the Church to the Roman Governor*, a work that as was customary entered its collections (inv. 48). The painting was chosen for the simplicity and fine rendering of the subject, "praiseworthy" for the representation of the context and the costumes faithful to the time period. However, the judgement was less benevolent regarding the execution of the figure with the basket and the "group of poor men", considered insufficiently "conspicuous".

On 15 April 1846, her appointment to the Ducale Accademia delle Belle Arti di Parma is recorded.

In 1850 she married the Riminese count Giovanni Battista Salducci.

Her name is listed among the artists who took part in the exhibitions of the Società degli amatori e cultori delle belle arti. Her presence is noted in 1867 with two works: *St James* and *St Agnes*; and again in 1869 with two pastel portraits and a third work entitled *A Sicilian Costume*.

In addition to the portraits for which she is known, the artist also received religious commissions, such as the *Ecstasy of Michele de' Santi* for San Carlo alle Quattro Fontane (1847), depicting the saint in the act of exchanging his heart for that of the Saviour. In 1867 she executed a painting for the chapel of the Pious Union of the Daughters of Mary, intended for the church of Sant'Agnese on the Via Nomentana.

The name Amalia De Angelis was also known outside Italy: we know of an *Apparition of the Virgin to St Stephen King of Hungary* (1870), destined for the church of the city of Brod in Croatia. A few years later, the painter executed a portrait from life of the bishop of Đakovoin, Slavonia (Croatia), Monsignor Strossmayer, destined for the lecture hall of the Accademia delle Scienze e delle Arti which he had helped to found in 1861.

De Angelis died in Rome in 1873: her funeral was held in the parish church of Santi Vincenzo e Anastasio a Trevi and her burial is registered as having taken place on 13 December of that year.

BIBLIOGRAPHY: Anna Lisa Genovese, "La premiazione nei concorsi gregoriani (1838–1874) delle pittrici Amalia de Angelis, Erminia Pompili e Luisa Bigioli." *Annali della Pontificia Insigne Accademia di Belle Arti e Lettere dei Virtuosi al Pantheon* 14 (2014), 362–73; Michela Gianfranceschi, "Diario 1837–1851." In Vitaliano Tiberia, *La Congregazione dei Virtuosi al Pantheon da Pio VII a Pio IX*. Galatina: Congedo, 2015, 360.

Alice Militello

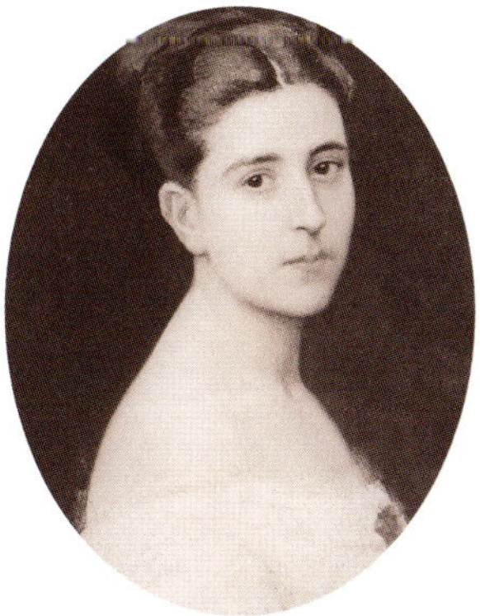

Erminia De Sanctis

(Rome, 1840–1919)

Erminia trained in Rome with her brother, the painter Guglielmo (Rome, 1829–1911), with whom she shared a studio in Via Margutta no. 33. In an article published in the magazine *La vita italiana*, the artist and writer Clotilde Ferrarini (Florence, 1869–?) describes the atmosphere felt on crossing the studio's entrance hall: "one cannot avoid being seized by a sense of religious admiration, which persuades us that we are within a temple of art". The Florentine painter also recalls the small studio "where we hear the light touch of feminine fingers, flowers, the prettiest flowers, painted with rare expertise by the delicate hand of Erminia, the inseparable and beloved sister of De Sanctis, whom he habitually introduces as the greatest comfort of his life". A photograph in Rome's Archivio Fotografico Comunale immortalizes the studio with Erminia, Guglielmo and some of his most famous works, including *Emanuele Filiberto Introducing His Son to Some Peasants* of 1872 (Rome, Quirinal collections, inv. SM 2-ODP 2529), copied by his sister in watercolour in 1887 Rome, Museo di Roma, inv. MR 44143).

Though Erminia's name was not particularly well-known in Rome, she participated in numerous exhibitions in Rome and Italy. In his *Dizionario*, Angelo De Gubernatis mentions Erminia in the biography of Emma Regis, recalling the submission of an illuminated parchment, decorated by both painters, "containing an address by the Women of Alexandria to their Majesties the king and queen" on the occasion of the Turin *Exhibition* of 1880. That the Regis and De Sanctis families were close is also attested by an undated note sent by Gioachino Regis to Guglielmo De Sanctis, accompanied by a "little medal of the great Mazzini who always wore a symbol of his slogan 'Rome or death'". The paper and the medal are now in the Historical Archive of the Ospedale degli Innocenti in Florence. In 1916, Guglielmo De Sanctis' numerous works and letters were donated to the Florentine museum at Erminia's wishes. She chose the prestigious Florentine institution to honour her brother, protecting his paintings from "sales not in keeping with their artistic value" and having them displayed in the special room of the gallery mentioned in the guidebooks as the *De Sanctis Room.*

Erminia specialized in the execution of copies and in genre painting, preferring the artistic techniques of watercolour and pastel. Specifically, she was a skilled copyist of some of the most famous paintings by her brother and other artists who frequented the studio in Via Margutta, including the well-known painter and friend Bernardo Celentano.

Bibliography: Agostino Mario Comanducci, *Dizionario illustrato pittori, e incisori italiani moderni e contemporanei.* 4 vols. 3rd edition. Milan: Patuzzi, 1962, 2:1196.

Michela D'Agostino

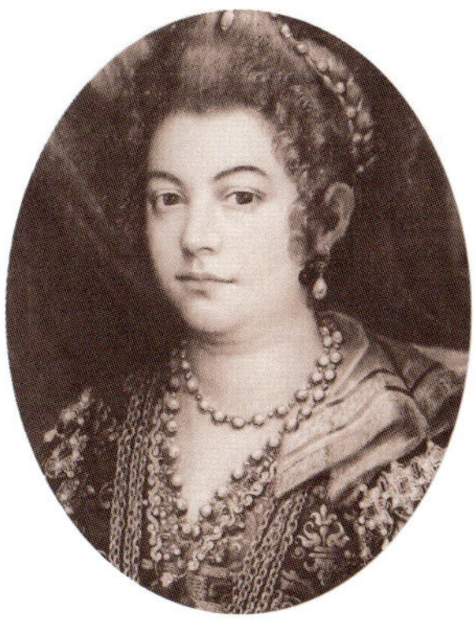

Claudia Del Bufalo

(Rome?, last quarter of the 16th century – early decades of the 17th century)

Claudia Del Bufalo was a painter active in Rome in the early decades of the 17th century, as attested by some references identified in the inventories of the Borghese and Savelli collections. Currently, her only known work is the signed painting depicting her sister, Faustina Del Bufalo, described in the inventory of the properties of Cardinal Scipione Borghese drawn up in around 1632. Observation

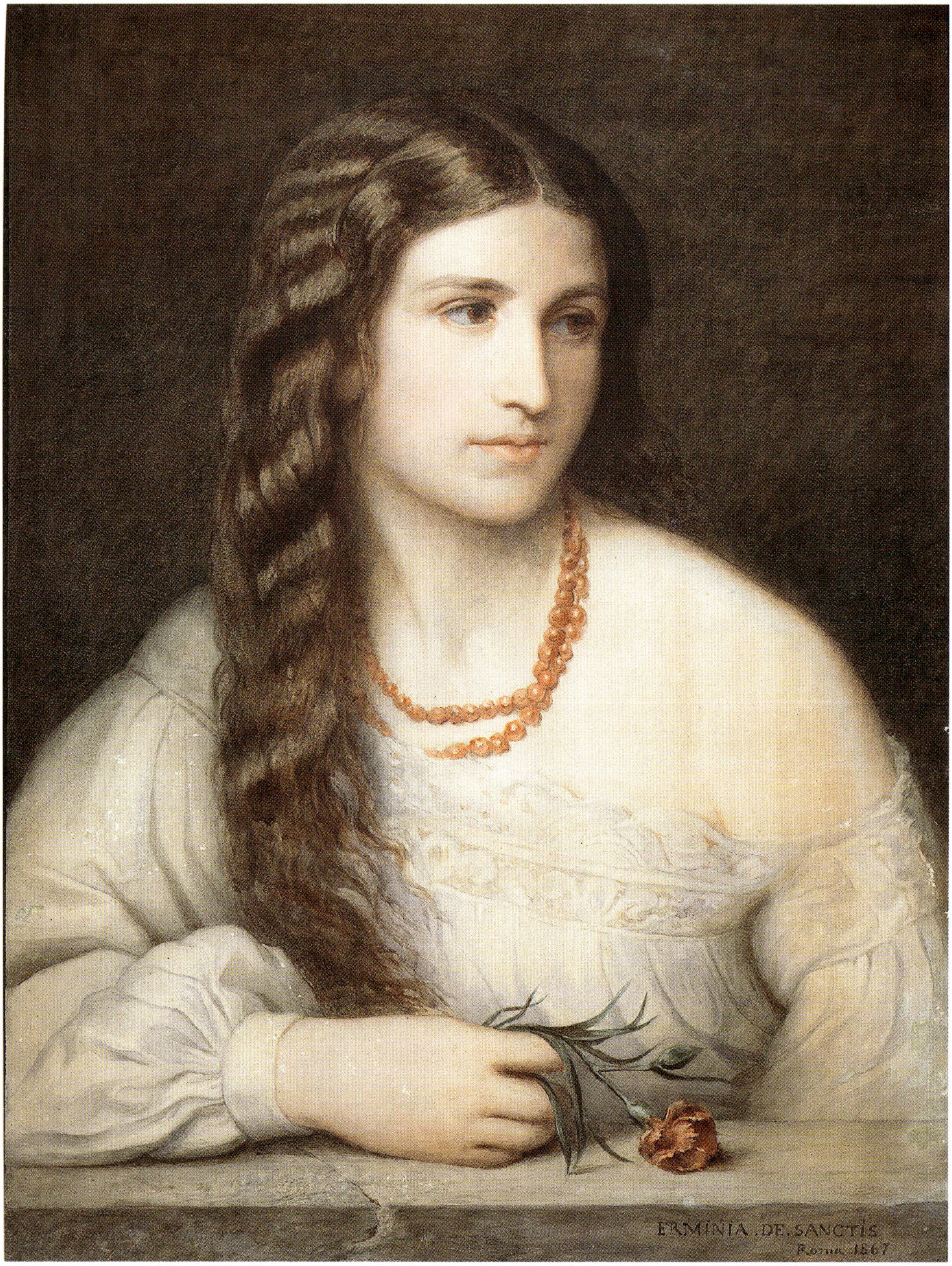

Erminia De Sanctis, *Portrait of Medora (Carolina Rapazzini)*, 1867. Private Collection.

Claudia Del Bufalo, *Portrait of Faustina Del Bufalo*, 1604. Rome, Dario Del Bufalo Collection.

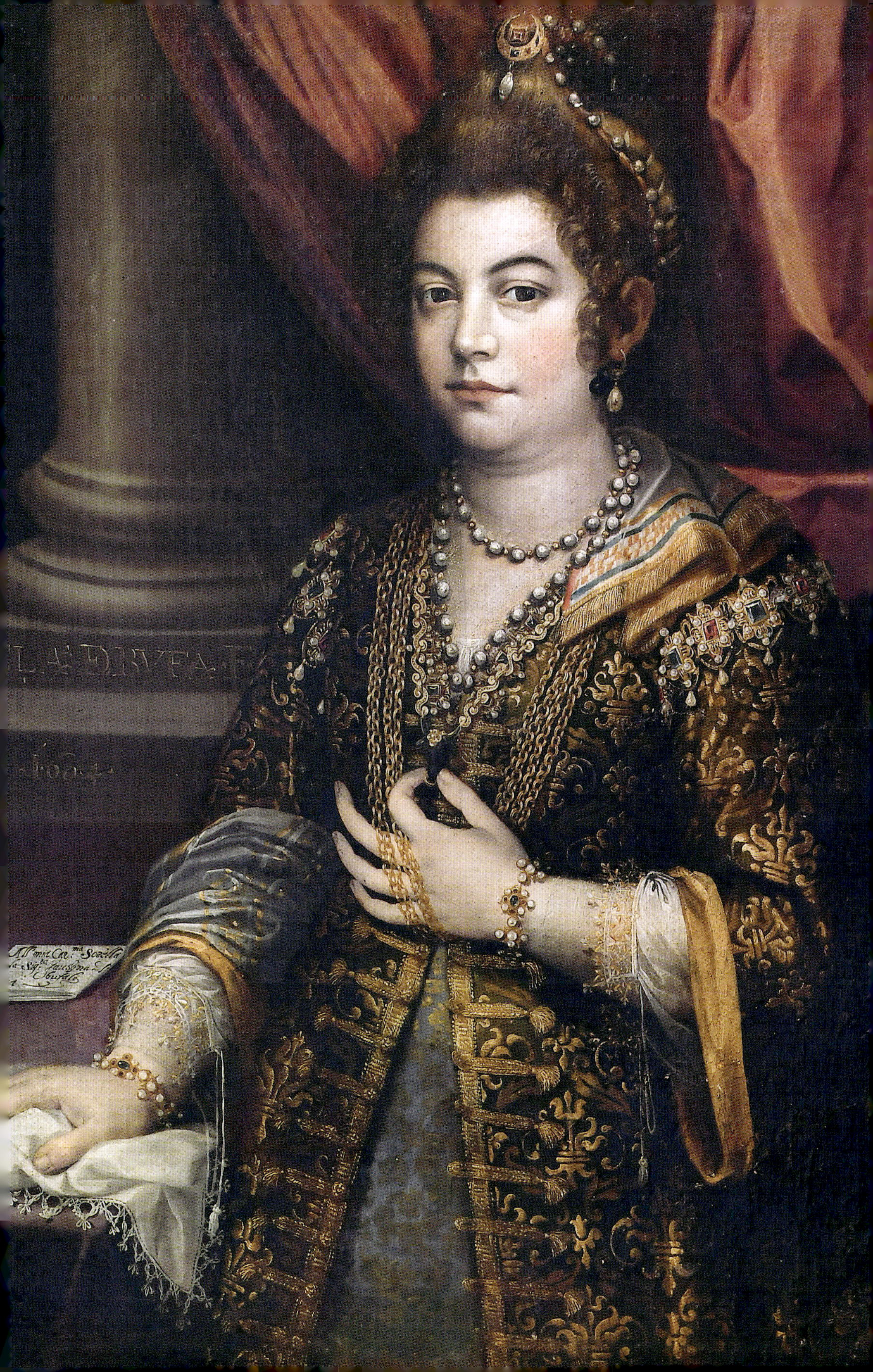
1604

of this portrait reveals that the painter must have possessed an in-depth knowledge of contemporary conventions of portraiture, though the circumstances under which she trained remain uncertain. It is unclear how the portrait of her sister came to be in the Borghese house; likewise, it is not known if the two Savelli paintings, "an Andromeda bound to the rock" and "a large painting representing the illustrious members of the family", were a gift from the painter or were executed on commission. The adjective "large" used to describe the portrait and the fact that it was later moved to the spacious hall of the palace at Ariccia suggest that it was held in high regard.

It has been suggested that Claudia and Faustina are pseudonyms of two of the three daughters of Quinzio Del Bufalo and Cassandra Strozzi, Silvia, Virginia and Dianora. However, it seems unlikely that the signature would not include the painter's baptismal name: for women artists, their own signature represented the only guarantee of recognition. Among the papers of the Del Bufalo archive we find traces of a Claudia Gironi, married to Orazio Del Bufalo and resident in Piazza Colonna, but there is insufficient information to establish whether she was the painter. The failure to include her maiden name in the signature in particular leads us to believe that she was not the Roman painter. The discovery of a marriage registered in 1583 between a Claudia Del Bufalo and Allegrino Delle Gemme at the parish church of Santa Maria in Publicolis opens up the possibility that she was a member of a different branch of the family. Additionally, the painter should probably be identified as the author of a sonnet and another poem published in 1609 in a collection by the French prelate Jacques Seguier.

BIBLIOGRAPHY: Ilaria Arcangeli, "Ricerche su Claudia Del Bufalo, pittrice nella Roma di primo Seicento." In *Rivista dell'Istituto Nazionale d'Archeologia e Storia dell'Arte* ser. 3, 46, no. 78 (2023), 301–9.

Ilaria Arcangeli

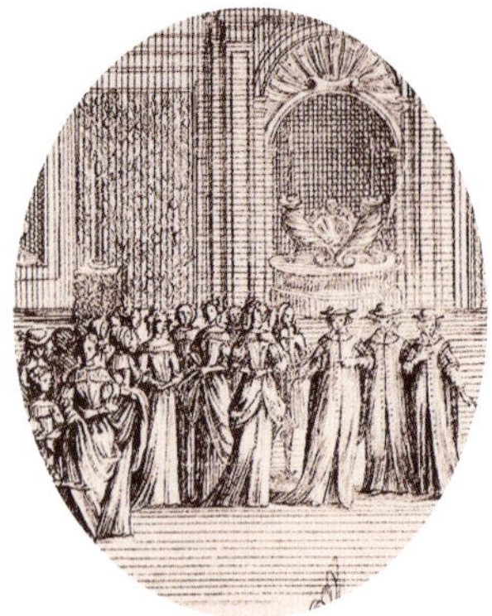

Teresa Del Po

(Rome, 1649 – Naples, 1713)

Teresa Del Po was born in 1649 in Rome, where her parents Pietro and Porzia Compagna had moved two years earlier, establishing profitable professional connections and friendships in the art world as demonstrated by the choice of her godfather, the sculptor Alessandro Algardi. The Del Po family settled in Via Margutta and it is here that Giacomo (1654–1726), Teresa, Anna Antonia (born in 1656) and Andrea (born in around 1643), the son of Porzia's first marriage, learned the rudiments of drawing and painting from their father (no information on this is available on Andriano, born in 1651). Andrea worked in theatre as a set designer and producer, while a miniature by the youngest daughter is recorded in the collection of Maffeo Barberini.

Teresa and Giacomo often worked together, especially in the production of prints drawn from various artists, including their father. While some paintings by her brother on religious subjects executed for various Roman churches are documented, Teresa was interested principally in miniatures and "gained renown in this sort of painting, towards which she felt a strong inclination; consequently, she was given as a teacher a foreigner who was an excellent miniaturist, who was living in Rome at the time and whose name I do not know. It is known only that Teresa was greatly charmed by his miniatures" (De Dominici). Other sources also fail to name this master, but his teachings were certainly fundamental for the artist, who was admitted to the Accademia di San Luca in 1675. Two years later she received a diploma, transcribed in the biographies of Lione Pascoli, in which she is described as "a highly diligent miniaturist and a very accurate printmaker in the etching technique". Her minia-

tures were present in the Barberini and Colonna collections, though their whereabouts are currently unknown. Some works have been attributed to her on their appearance on the art market. Her work as a miniaturist was accompanied by that as a printmaker: as already reconstructed by the studies, her production in Rome consisted principally of illustrations for printed books, alongside loose prints based on works by her father and his circle. A noteworthy example is the *Head of John the Baptist* (Rome, Istituto Centrale per la Grafica, inv. S-FC30946), after a drawing by Angelica Roncalli, on which no information has hitherto emerged.
Following her tempestuous separation from her husband Muzio Virgili, whom she had married in 1678, Teresa moved definitively to Naples in 1683 with the entire Del Po family. Here she obtained large numbers of commissions, working in the pastel technique in addition to continuing her prolific activity as an engraver.

BIBLIOGRAPHY: Donata Minonzio, "Teresa Del Po." In *Italian Masters of the Seventeenth Century. Commentary*, ed. by Paolo Bellini, Richard W. Wallace. Pleasantville: Abaris Books, 1990, 267–332; Paola Toscano, "Teresa del Po: alcune stampe inedite." *Grafica d'arte* 19, no. 75 (2008), 5–9.

Ilaria Arcangeli

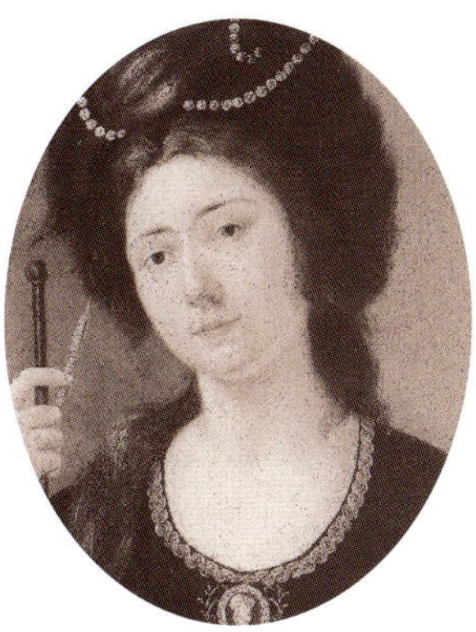

Irene Duclos Parenti

(Florence?, *c.* 1754–1795)

Based on the inscription on the back of her *Self-Portrait* in the Gallerie degli Uffizi (inv. 1890 no. 5556), Irene was the daughter of Giovan Battista Duclos, about whom very little is known. Of a different opinion is Sheila Barker, who thinks her the daughter of the modest painter Giuseppe Parenti, active at Fucecchio, married in 1768 to the unknown Giovan Battista Duclos who died before 1783. Also uncertain are the date – around 1754 – and place of her birth – Florence – given the presumed lack of documentary evidence. She is known to have had a long career as a copyist, mainly in Florence starting from 1773, the year in which her first request for permission to copy portraits and famous works by the old masters kept in the Gallerie degli Uffizi was accepted. She continued this occupation regularly until 1779, when, a clear marker of her talents as a painter, she executed for Grand Duke Pietro Leopoldo a faithful oil on canvas copy of Andrea del Sarto's 1525 fresco of the *Madonna del Sacco* (Florence, Galleria dell'Accademia, OdA Pitti 333) in the cloister of the Basilica of the Santissima Annunziata. Aside from the *Portrait of the Jesuit Abbot Joseph Hilarius Eckhel* of 1773 (Florence, Gallerie degli Uffizi, inv. 1890 no. 311) commissioned by the then director of the Gallery Raimondo Cocchi, during those six years Irene executed a total of thirty-nine paintings, counting only the copies, in response to specific requests, particularly from a growing number of foreign buyers. Her sojourn in Rome dates to the years between 1780 and 1782 and, though linked to her activity as a poetess of the Arcadian Academy under the pseudonym of Lincasta Ericinia, must have represented the pinnacle of her artistic career: in the following year she was elected member of the Accademia del Disegno in Florence and of the Accademia di San Luca in Rome. She also devoted herself to encaustic painting, assisted by the chemist Giovanni Fabbroni. In 1786, her name was inscribed in the register of honorary members of the Accademia Clementina. With the exception of the eloquent pages devoted to her by Vicente Requeno in 1787, Duclos' final years have not yet been studied in depth. She died in 1795, probably in Florence.

BIBLIOGRAPHY: Sheila Barker *et al.*, *Irene Parenti Duclos. A Work Restored, An Artist Revealed. / Un'Opera Restaurata, un'Artista Rivelata.* Prato: B' Gruppo, 2011.

Isabella Colucci

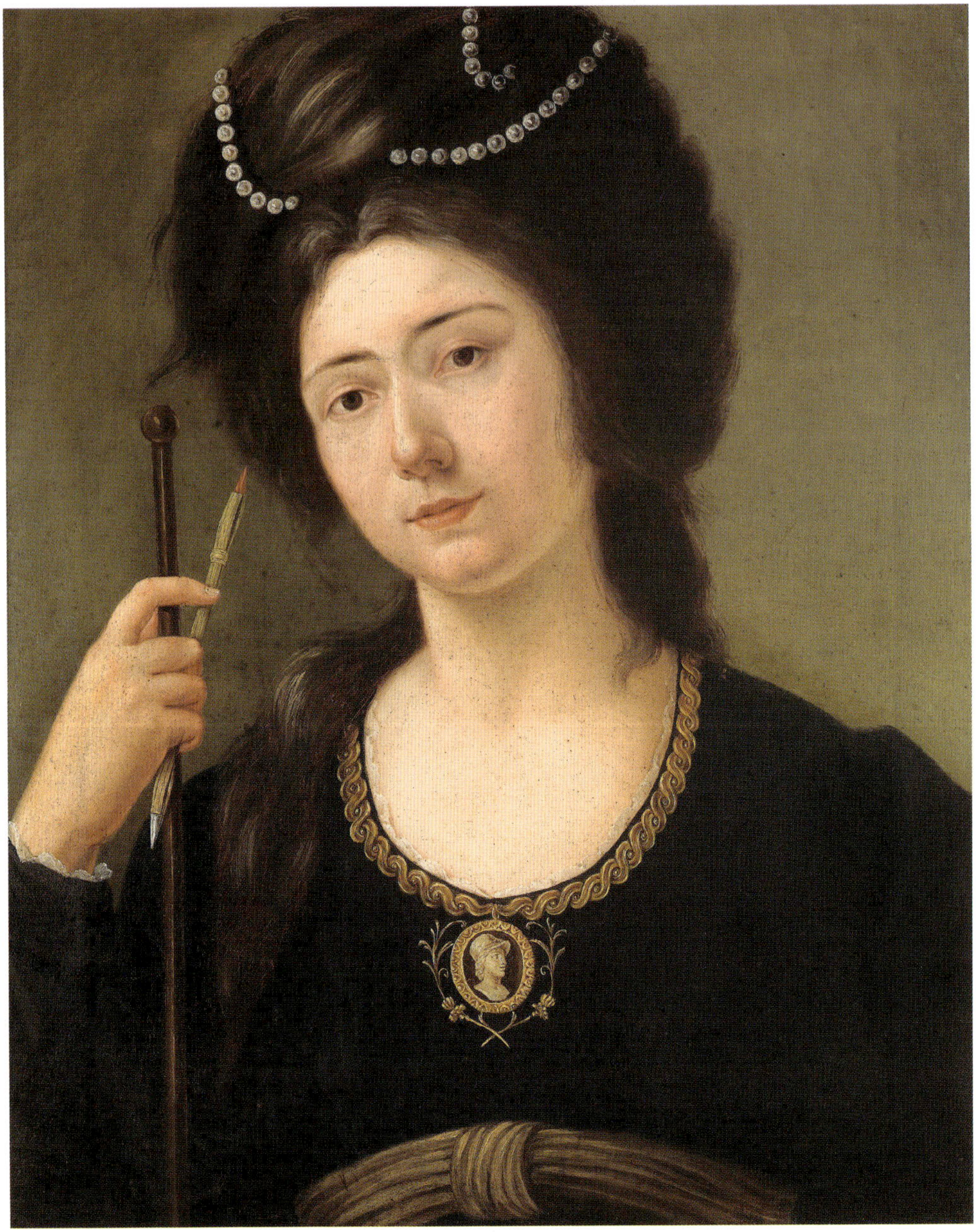

 Irene Duclos Parenti, *Self-Portrait*, 1783. Florence, Gallerie degli Uffizi.

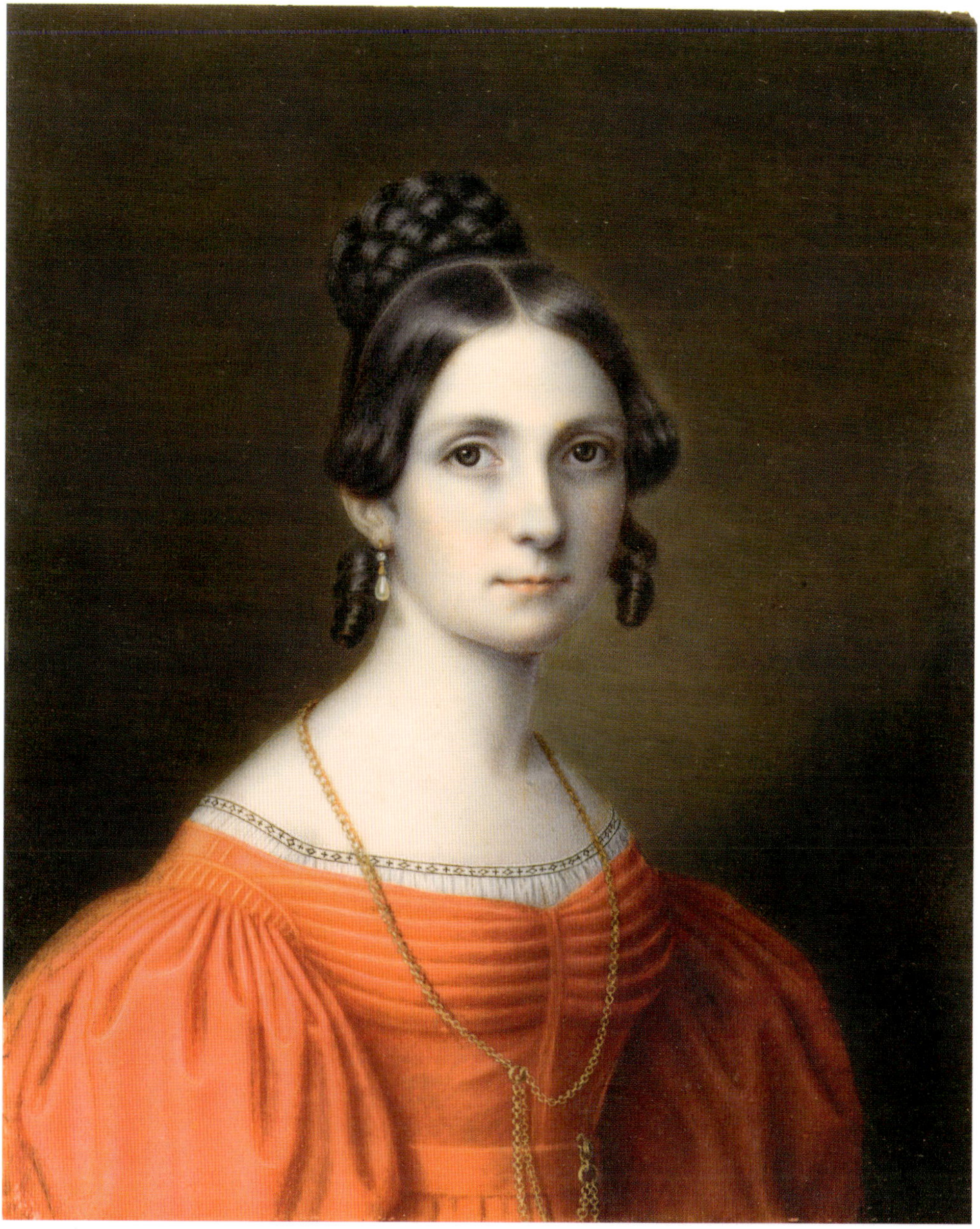

Teresa Fioroni (Voigt), *Self-Portrait*, 1837. Rome, Accademia Nazionale di San Luca.

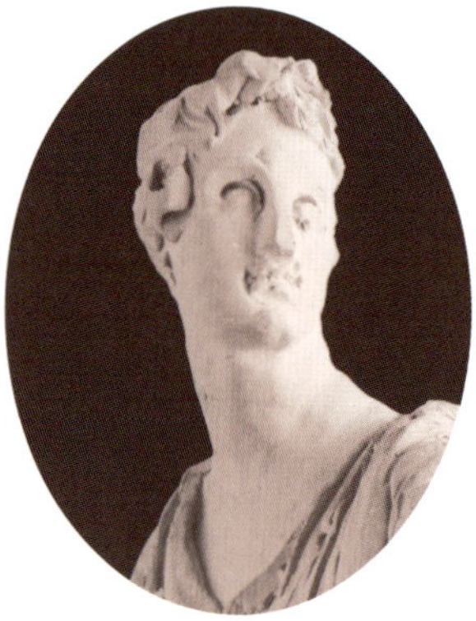

Leopoldine Esterházy

(Vienna, 1788 – Libeschitz, 1846)

Leopoldine Esterházy was the second child of Prince Nikolaus II Esterházy (1765–1833) and of Maria Hermenegilde Liechtenstein (1768–1845). Her education, encouraged by her parents and in line with aristocratic customs, focused on languages, literature, music and painting. "Endowed with every beauty, adorned with every grace", as Isabella Teotochi Albrizzi wrote of her, from a young age the princess showed a precocious interest in her father's renowned drawing collection kept in the castle at Eisenstadt and a particular fondness for landscape painting, probably thanks to her association with Eduard Gurk, Joseph Fischer and Albert Dies, artists working at her father's court. This passion for the arts is documented both by contemporary sources and by two art works: a landscape with ruins (1803, Esterházy Privatstiftung, Schloss Eisenstadt, Grafische Sammlung, presumably identifiable as that mentioned in the manuscript catalogue of the Esterházy collection, Budapest, Szépművészeti Múzeum) and a river landscape in the Museo Civico of Bassano del Grappa signed and dated September 1805 (inv. Dis.Bass.2.80 2.80.176). In the summer of that same year Leopoldine began a relationship with Maurice of Liechtenstein, her future husband and the person who introduced her to Antonio Canova, who was in Vienna at the time for the unveiling of the monument to Maria Christina of Austria. Having travelled to Eisenstadt on invitation from the Esterházy family, the sculptor "became better acquainted with the young princess Leopoldina, praised her drawings and became so captivated by her grace and love of art that he promised to immortalize her in a portrait". Her connections with the art world in Rome, which the princess must have visited earlier with her father – who usually spent the winter in the city, where his sister had a famous salon – and later with her husband, are attested by a well-known letter sent from Wurzburg in 1821 after the delivery of the statue. In the missive, the princess expresses her gratitude for the sculpture and makes a significant reference to the *Sleeping Nymph* on which Canova was working at the time. Confirming her interest in Canova's work and more generally in events in the Roman art world, she then expresses the hope of soon seeing the city and the sculptor again: "Rome and you, my dear Canova, are both carved on my heart and I am hopeful that the day might come on which I shall see you both again" (letter of 21 December 1821 from Leopoldine to Canova). She signed the letter simply Leopoldine Lichtenstein, a sign of affection and familiarity.

bibliography: Ingeborg Schemper-Sparholz, "'Le désir d'avoir la nature en marbre': die Sitzstatue der Prinzessin Leopoldine Esterházy-Liechtenstein von Antonio Canova und das Frauenbild der Frühromantik." *Wiener Jahrbuch für Kunstgeschichte* L (1997), 255–95; I. Schemper-Sparholz, in *Canova e la Venere vincitrice*, exhib. cat. (Rome 2007–8), ed. by Anna Coliva, Fernando Mazzocca. Milan: Electa, 2007, 250–53.

Jessica Calipari

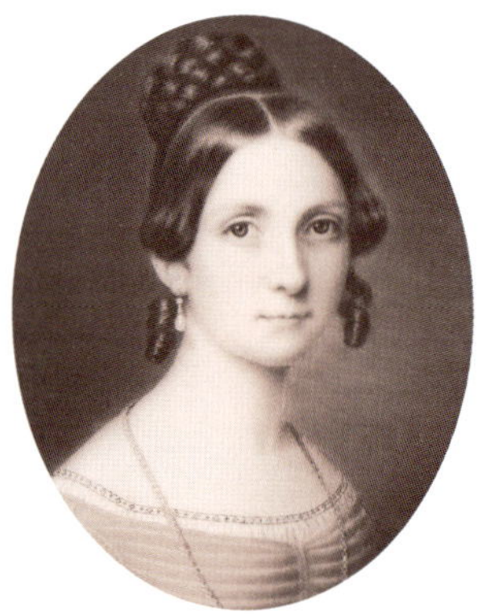

Teresa Fioroni (Voigt)

(?, 1799 – Perugia, 1880)

The Fioroni moved, perhaps directly from Santa Fiora in Tuscany where they were living, to Rome and no. 68 Via Sistina, in an area popular with artists like Bertel Thorvaldsen and the Nazarenes. This was thus a fortunate location for Teresa, a miniaturist, and her brother, Luigi, a painter. Teresa learned the art of miniature painting from Domenico del Frate, a painter from Lucca who lived with the Fioroni family as a tenant during the final years of his life. Though highly educated, the family must have belonged to the lower middle class as the children were forced to work to help with household expenses. On 30 March 1830, Teresa married Carl-Friederich Voigt of Berlin, a medallist and gem-engraver, and the same year followed him to Munich where he was employed at the mint. Before marrying, she signed her miniatures with her maiden name, while from 1830 she used only her married name. Equally, she worked full time while still in Rome, but after becoming a mother spent less time on painting, despite what she said in a letter to her family of 1849: "my beloved miniature painting, such a comfort to me". Her correspondence with her family during the Munich years represents an important source for understanding the artist and her work, not just as a painter but also as a businesswoman. This is evident from the advice given to her sister Enrichetta, urging her to deal carefully with clients, asking neither too much nor too little for a miniature, and encouraging her to visit some galleries as this might be "very useful". After many years far from home, her nostalgia for Rome became so intense that she ascribed her physical problems to this separation; in a letter to her sister Angelina of 13 January 1846, she reports her husband Carl's words: "We must return to Rome [...] Roman women cannot live without frequent visits to their hometown". In 1857 she finally returned to the city with her husband and children, settling first in Via delle Tre Cannelle and then in Via della Croce until 1874, the year of Carl Friederich's death in Trieste. Teresa then moved to Perugia, where she died in 1880. Of her miniatures on ivory, mostly portraits, the majority are in the Accademia di San Luca; others are in private collections or known only from the literature.

BIBLIOGRAPHY: P. Di Natale, in *Da Raffaello a Balla. Capolavori dell'Accademia Nazionale di San Luca*, exhib. cat. (Bard 2017–18), ed. by Vittorio Sgarbi, Francesco Moschini, Bard: Forte di Bard, 2017, 202–7.

Laura Palombaro

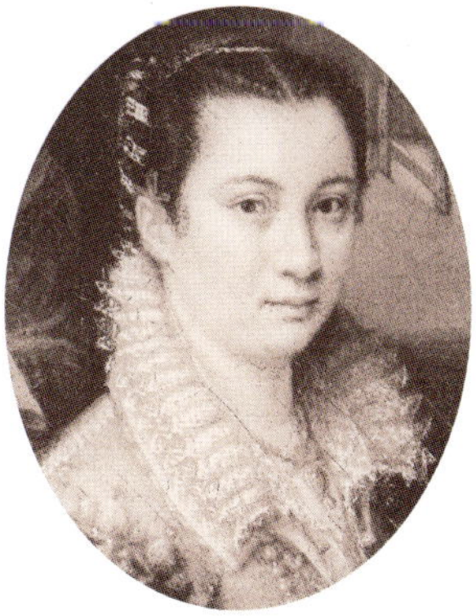

Lavinia Fontana

(Bologna, 1552 – Rome, 1614)

The daughter of the well-known painter Prospero Fontana (Bologna, 1512–1597), Lavinia Fontana began her artistic career in Bologna in her father's workshop. Even before moving permanently to Rome in 1604, she obtained numerous commissions from cultured individuals in the city. In a letter of 17 October 1578, Alfonso Chacón, a Dominican theologian and prominent exponent of post-Tridentine politics, commissioned "a small portrait of yourself" from her to add to his collection of portraits of famous men and women. Lavinia accepted the task on 3 May 1579 and executed the *Self-Portrait in the Studio* now in the Gallerie degli Uffizi (inv. 1890, 4013). In two letters sent on 3 November and 12 December of the same year, the historian Carlo Sigonio mentions the portrait executed for him by the painter, later sent to the Roman scholar Fulvio Orsini. This work, originally identified as the portrait in the Museo Civico of Modena, is now recognized as the painting on copper discovered in 2009 on the art market (London, Christie's, 8 July 2009, lot 244). In 1600, she executed for Cardinal Girolamo Bernerio the *Altarpiece of St Hyacinth*, destined for the chapel dedicated to the saint in the church of Santa Sabina where it can still be seen today.

Lavinia is documented in Rome for the first time in a letter from Virginio Roberti of 28 April 1604, as the guest of Cardinal Alessandro d'Este at his residence in Palazzo Salviati on Via della Lungara. The reason was the contract signed on 19 February 1603, unbeknownst to the painter herself, by her husband Giovanni Paolo Zappi in the presence of Cardinal Bernerio and of the abbot of San Paolo Fuori le Mura, for the altarpiece with the *Stoning of St Stephen* destined for the basilica. The work was destroyed in the

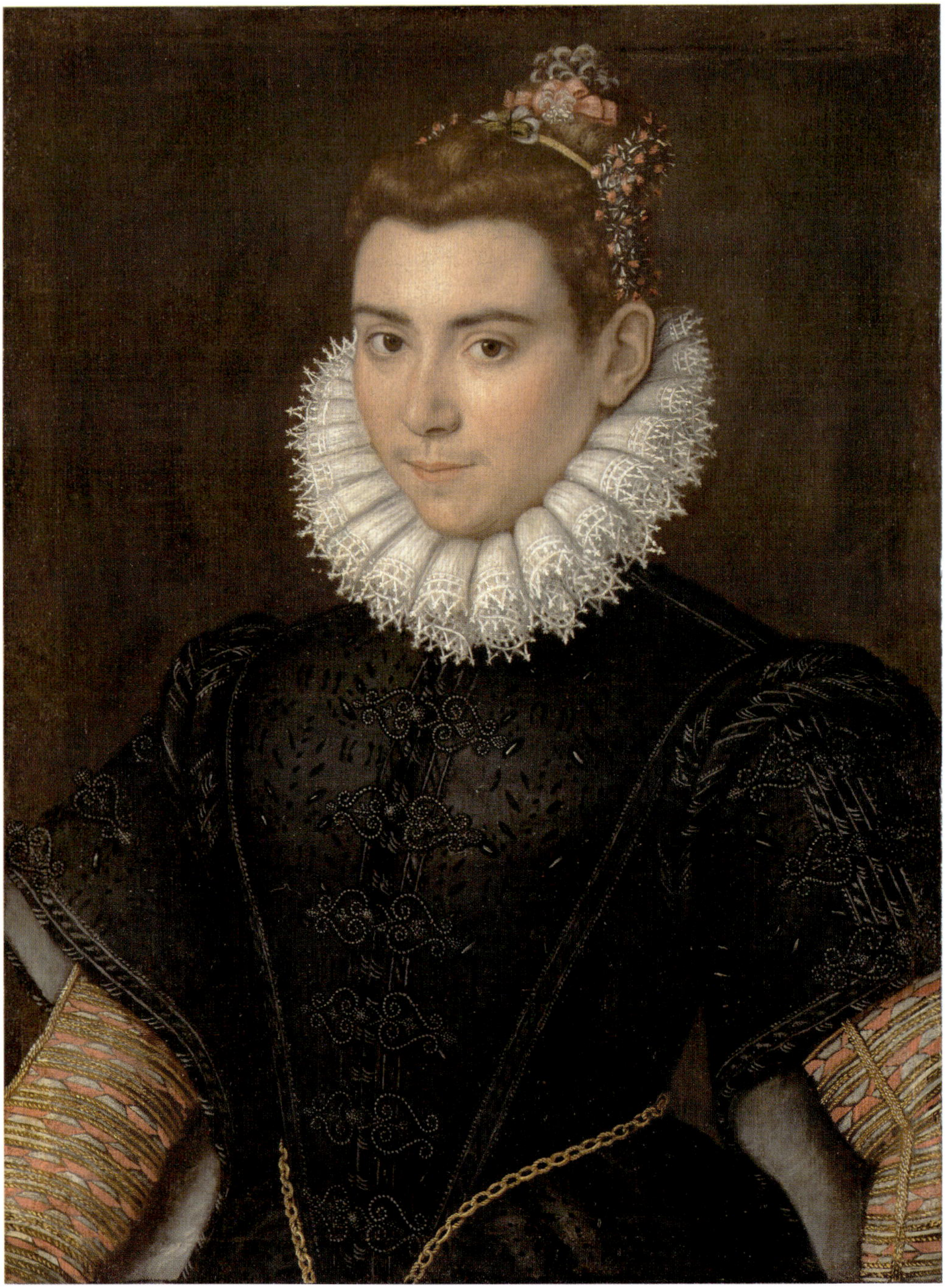

Lavinia Fontana, *Portrait of a Young Aristocratic Woman*, c. 1590-1600. Private Collection.

Emma Gaggiotti (Richards), *The Gaggiotti Richards Family*, c. 1853.
Rome, Museo di Roma, Gabinetto delle Stampe (detail).

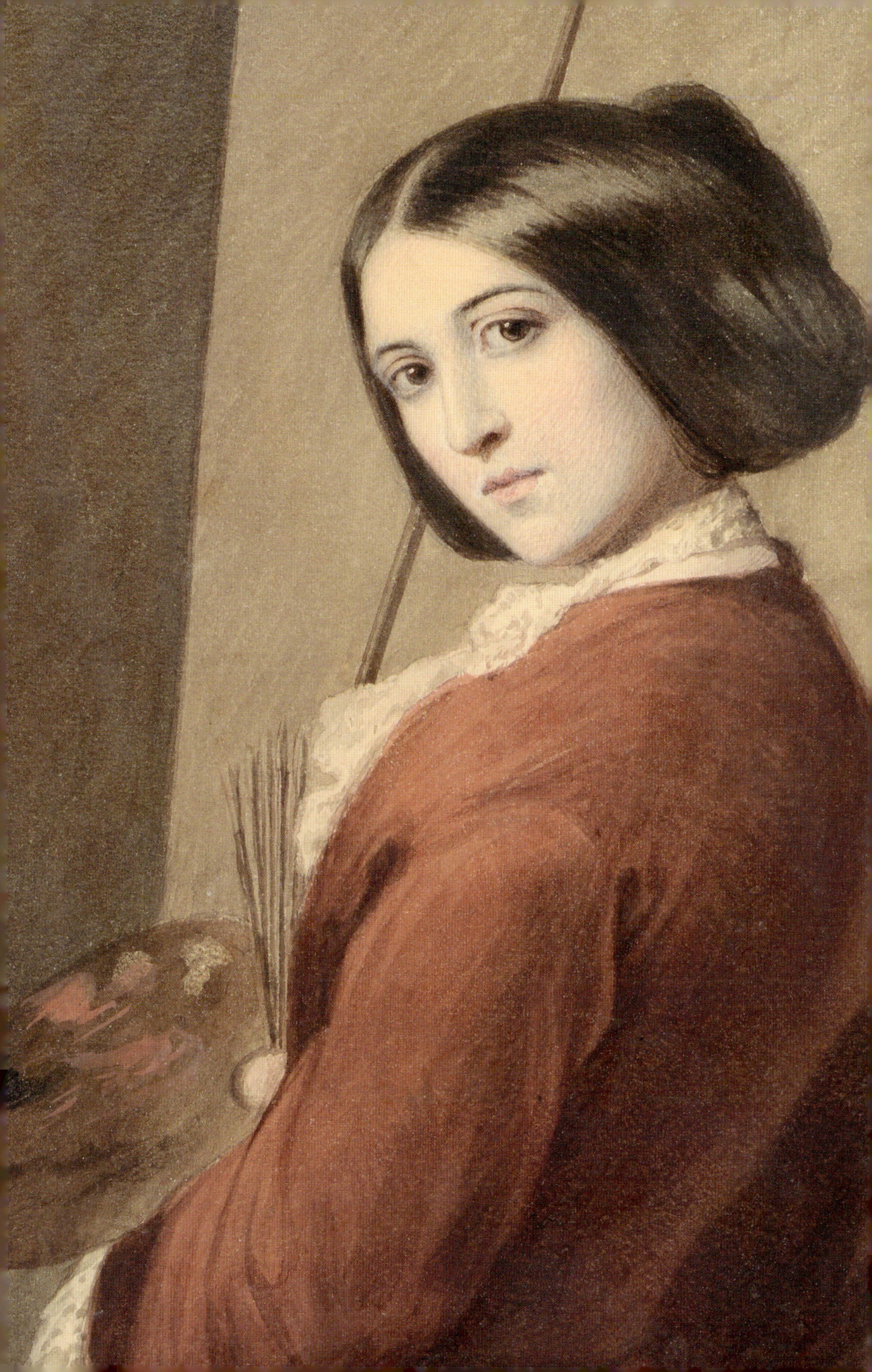

fire of 1823 but is known thanks to the engraving by Jacques Callot (New York, The Metropolitan Museum of Art, inv. 59.569.2). Although no documents have been found attesting to Fontana's presence at the Accademia di San Luca, the artistic literature (from Giovanni Baglione to Filippo Baldinucci, via Marcello Oretti) allows us to assume that the painter was accepted at the distinguished Roman institute shortly after her arrival in Rome and that she donated one of her self-portraits, which has since disappeared. Between 1611 and 1614 she painted the four female saints on slate in Santa Maria della Pace for the nobleman Gaspare Rivaldi. In the *Avvisi urbinati* it is said that on 16 September 1609, Paul V gave the Persian ambassador a portrait of himself executed by the artist. In 1613, she painted the canvas with *Minerva Dressing* for Cardinal Scipione Borghese, now in the Galleria Borghese (inv. 007). In her death notice published in the *Avvisi urbinati* on 13 August she is remembered as a "painter unique among the women of our age, the equal of the greatest men in that profession".

BIBLIOGRAPHY: Maria Teresa Cantaro, *Lavinia Fontana bolognese "pittora singolare", 1552-1614.* Milan: Jandi Sapi, 1989; Ead., "Alcune novità su Lavinia Fontana dall'esordio al 1590 circa." *Bollettino d'arte* ser. 7, 106, nos. 51–2 (2021), 69–98; Raffaella Morselli, *Professione pittore. Il caso Bologna tra Cinque e Seicento.* Venice: Marsilio, 2022, 142–47.

Michela D'Agostino

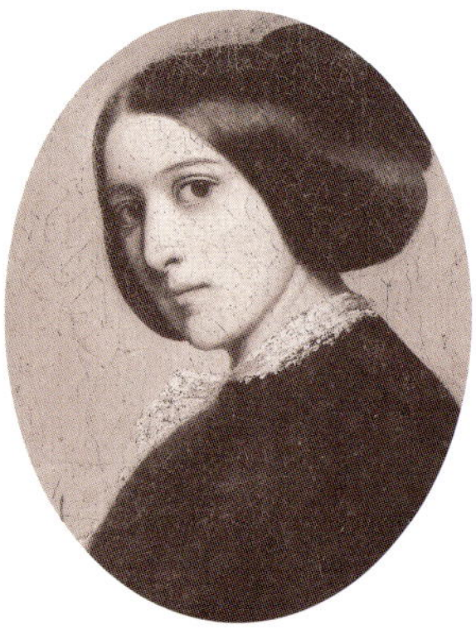

Emma Gaggiotti (Richards)

(Rome, 1825 – Velletri, 1912)

Emma Gaggiotti began her artistic career in Ancona under the guidance of the Purist painter Nicola Consoni, and later perfected her skills in Rome in the studio of Tommaso Minardi. Francesco Hayez's memoirs (*Le mie memorie*), published posthumously, include a drawing "executed during his stay in Rome" portraying Emma, though the year of execution is not specified. Further evidence that the two artists were close is the *Portrait of Angiolina Gaggiotti* (the painter's mother) executed by Hayez in 1834 and now lost. Emma Gaggiotti was known in Rome as an ardent patriot, to the extent that she was chosen by the war commission to canvas for support and donations from the Roman people in aid of the Italian troops. She moved to London after her marriage to the journalist Alfred Bate Richards in 1848. In 1851 she participated in the exhibition organized by the Royal Academy of Art, displaying six paintings including the *Portrait of a Lady.* The work drew the attention of Queen Victoria, who commissioned a self-portrait from her, executed in 1853 and now in the Royal Collection in London (inv. RCIN 408920). There is another version in the Galleria Palatina in Florence, formerly ascribed to the painter Rosa Bonheur (Bordeaux, 1822 – Thomery, 1899) but reattributed after conservation work in 2010 uncovered the signature of Emma Gaggiotti. In an article of 1853 Quirino Leoni wrote that during her time in London the painter kept up her contacts with Rome, sending a *Portrait of the Gaggiotti Family* (Rome, Museo di Roma, Gabinetto delle Stampe, MR 45594) to Giuseppe Massani, a close family friend "so that he could satisfy his gaze all at once with the semblances of so many loved ones far away". From the *Guida Monaci* we learn that she lived in Rome in Via Gregoriana no. 5 in 1872 and in 1875. Her gifts as a painter and musician were renowned in Rome and praised in poems by Leoni in 1855 and by Giuseppe Gioacchino Belli in 1865. After moving several times between Ancona and Florence, she settled in Velletri, where she died in 1912.

BIBLIOGRAPHY: Petra Gentz Werner, *Das Schweigen der Venus. Die Malerin Emma Gaggiotti-Richards (1825–1912) zwischen Alexander von Humboldt und König Wilhelm I.* Berlin: Trafo, 2018.

Michela D'Agostino

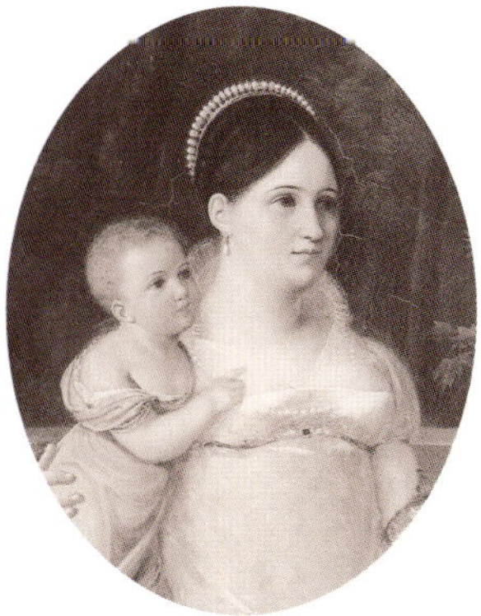

CARLOTTA GARGALLI
(Bologna, 1788 – Rome, 1840)

In *Italy*, the Irish writer Lady Morgan, pseudonym of Sidney Owenson, described Carlotta Gargalli as "the Elisabetta Sirani of the day". After her initial training with her father Filippo, a portraitist, 1804 Carlotta studied at the Accademia Nazionale di Belle Arti in Bologna. The first woman ever admitted, she took this chance to open up further opportunities for herself: she won a bursary to study at the Accademia del Regno Italico in Palazzo Venezia in Rome. This institution, founded by Giuseppe Tamboni and Antonio Canova, hosted students from three Italian academies of art, in Milan, Bologna and Venice. In 1811 Carlotta thus moved to Rome with her father. Her years in the city were difficult, burdened by the lack of money and hindered by the negative judgements of the Bolognese teachers, opposed to the novelties of Roman classicism. Nonetheless, this was a supportive and stimulating environment for Carlotta. She met Pelagio Palagi, Giovan Battista Bassi, Tommaso Minardi, Bianca Milesi and Francesco Hayez. Canova, her supporter, praised her works and allowed her to visit his own collection from which she drew several copies, like the *Portrait of an Ecclesiastic by Moretto* (Munich, Alte Pinakothek, inv. WAF 683). In 1815 she returned to Bologna, where four years later she was elected an honorary member of the Accademia. In 1821 she married Carlo Rovinetti, with whom she had Sofia; her married life also encouraged her to devote herself to restoration, a more remunerative activity. However, her professional successes were accompanied by grief over deaths in her family, culminating in that of Sofia in 1836. Six months later she married her second husband Antonio Bassi, a furniture seller and cabinetmaker. The *Almanacco letterario* or *Grande raccolta di 10000 indirizzi, ed altre interessanti notizie dell'interno di Roma* reports that in 1841 in Rome the two owned "a painting studio with copies after Raphael, Correggio and Guido Reni etc." in Via del Corso no. 63. Among the paintings executed during her years of study at Palazzo Venezia, the test pieces for her first, third and fourth years as a student survive: the aforementioned copy after Moretto, the *Ajax Taking Refuge on a Rock* (Bologna, Museo Ottocento, in storage at Palazzo Malvezzi, headquarters of the Province of Bologna, inv. 1053) and the *Pyrrhus Threatens Andromache To Kill Her Son Astyanax* (Bologna, Pinacoteca Nazionale, inv. 1049).

BIBLIOGRAPHY: *Carlotta Gargalli 1788-1840. Una pittrice bolognese nella Roma di Canova*, exhib. cat. (Bologna 2023), ed. by Ilaria Chia, Francesca Sinigaglia. Bologna: MiG, 2023.

Laura Palombaro

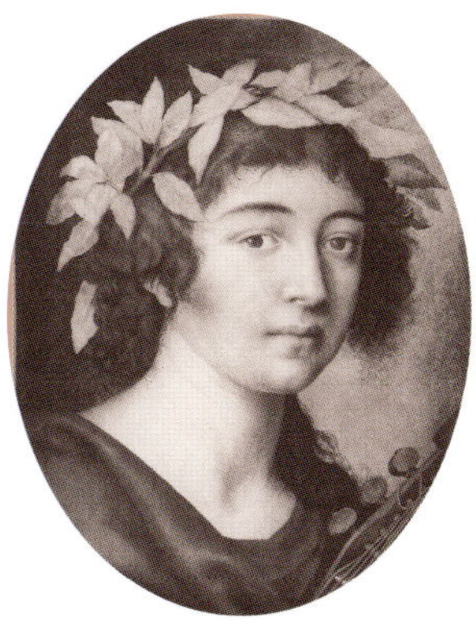

GIOVANNA GARZONI
(Ascoli Piceno, 1600 – Rome, 1670)

Originally from the Marche region, Giovanna Garzoni attained unprecedented renown in the art of miniature painting, working for numerous patrons and courts and establishing professional and personal relationships with intellectuals and artists. As her family originally came from Venice, she spent her youth there, making a close study of the works of Jacopo Palma the Younger and taking calligraphy lessons at the school of Giacomo Rogni. Her earliest miniatures date to her first stay in Florence (*c.* 1618–1620), when she almost certainly met Artemisia Gentileschi. She is again documented in

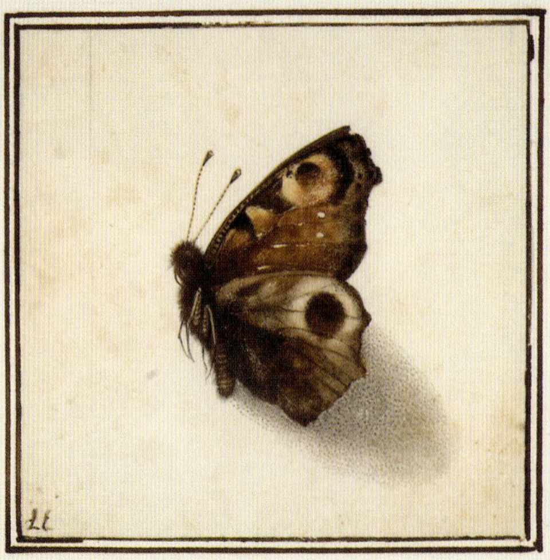

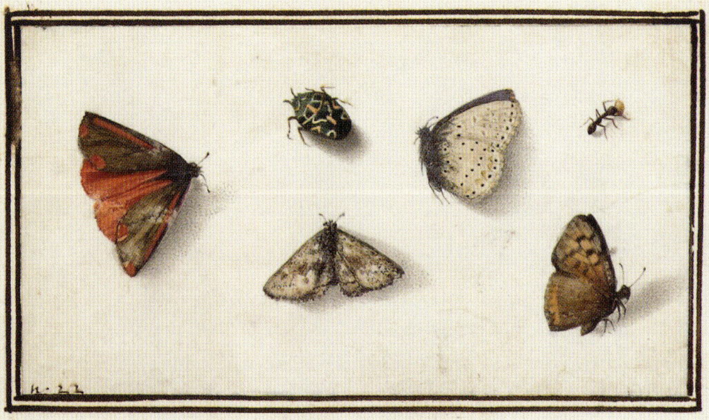

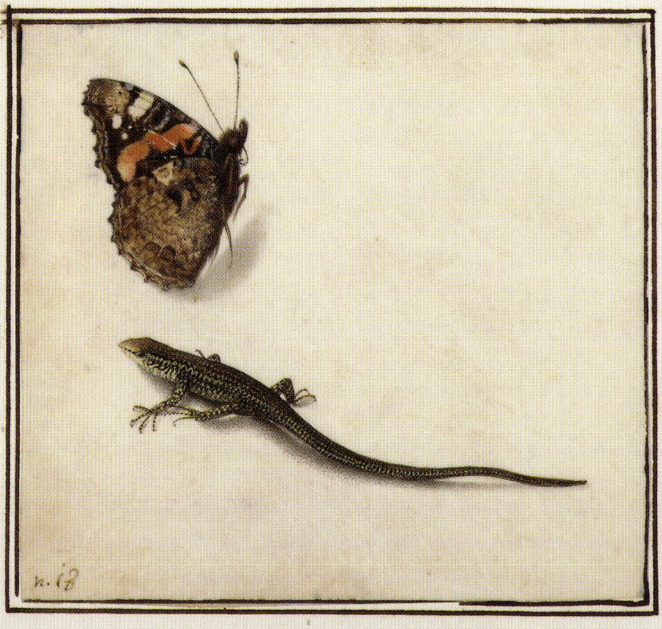

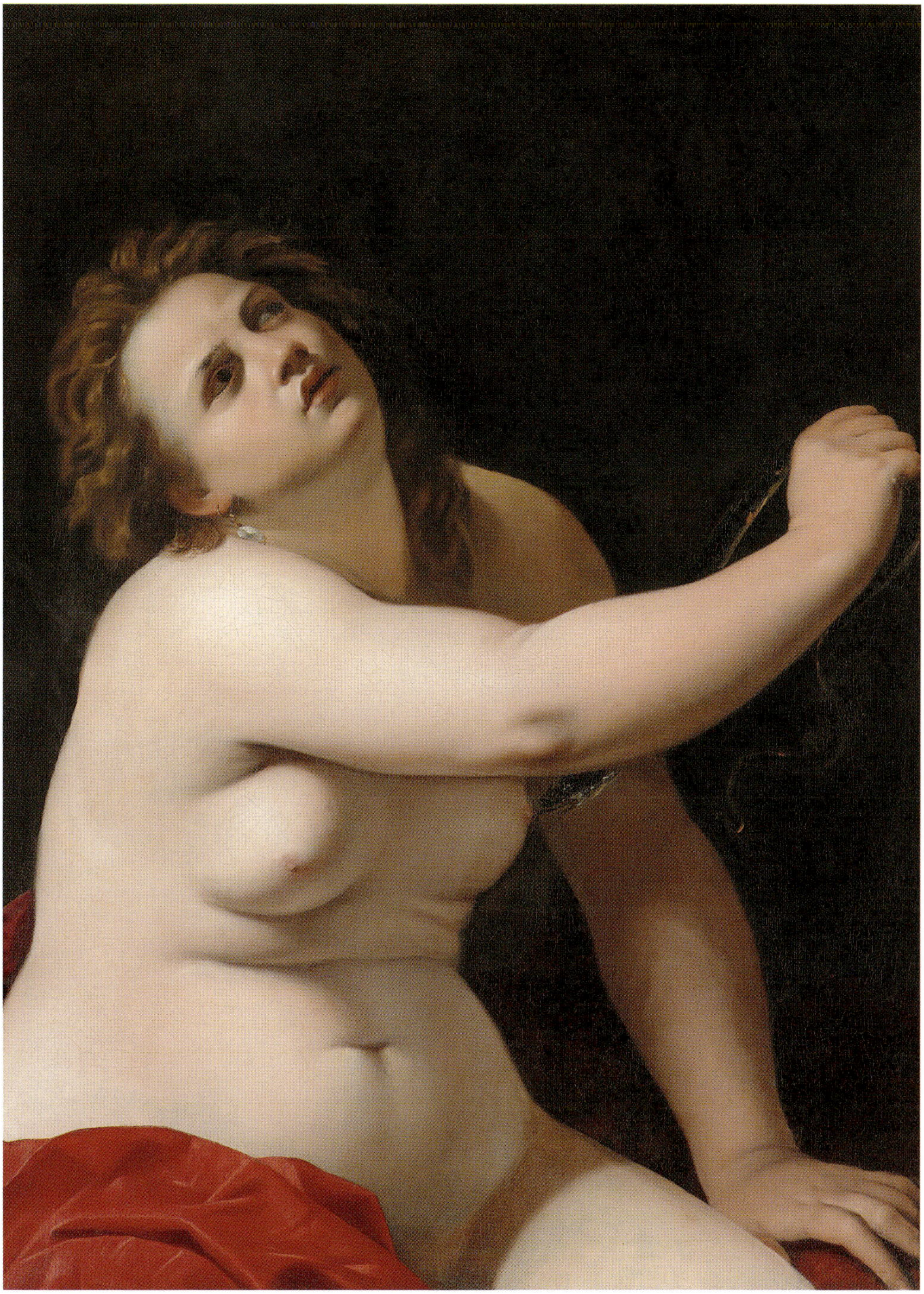

Giovanna Garzoni, *Album of Miniatures*, c. 1640. Rome, Accademia Nazionale di San Luca, Collezioni Disegni e Stampe.

Artemisia Gentileschi, *Cleopatra*, c. 1620. Ferrara, Fondazione Cavallini-Sgarbi.

Venice in 1625, when she executed the *Portrait of a Gentleman* (The Hague, Stichting Historische Verzamelingen van het Huis Oranje-Nassau, inv. MI-615). Before arriving in Naples in 1630, where she entered the service of the viceroy Fernando Afán de Ribera, she spent some time in Rome and came into contact with Cassiano dal Pozzo and the circle of naturalists connected to the Accademia dei Lincei. In a letter of 1631 written to Cassiano himself, the artist explicitly asked him for help in seeking new patrons in the city, since "my wish is to live and die in Rome" (Naples, 19 April 1631). But even this second stay did not last long: from the summer of 1632 she was in Turin at the invitation of Christine of France, Duchess of Savoy. She is listed on 3 April 1633 among the artists admitted to the Accademia di San Luca, though the authenticity of this document has in the past been questioned due to the presence of later additions. In any case, Garzoni's acknowledged success at this date would fully justify her election. Towards the end of 1637 she left Turin, perhaps returning to Rome in 1638 before departing for England and France. In 1642 she was again in the service of the Medici court, executing a large number of works. Starting in 1651 she settled in the papal city, consolidating her relationship with the circles of the Roman Accademia. She donated her personal archive and two albums to this institution. Her ties to Rome and the Accademia were definitively sanctioned by the construction of her funerary monument on the internal façade of the church of Santi Luca e Martina, dedicated to artists, next to which she had lived in a house that she had had built against its walls.

BIBLIOGRAPHY: Gerardo Casale, *Giovanna Garzoni. 'Insigne miniatrice'*. Milan: Jandi Sapi, 1991; *La grandezza dell'universo nell'arte di Giovanna Garzoni*, exhib. cat. (Florence 2020), ed. by Sheila Barker. Leghorn: Sillabe, 2020.

Ilaria Arcangeli

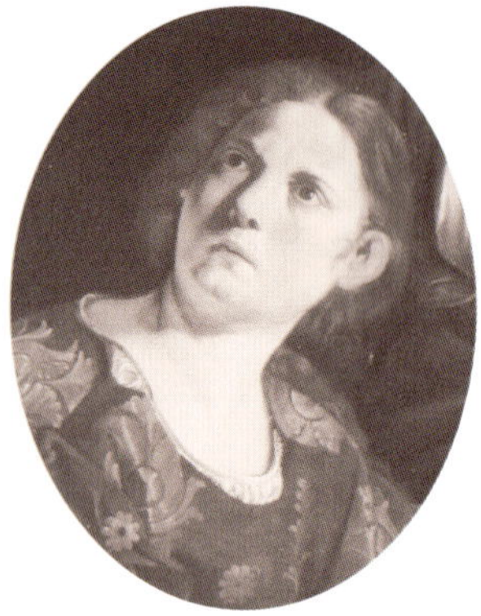

Artemisia Gentileschi

(Rome, 1593 – Naples?, after 1654)

Rome played a crucial role in Artemisia Gentileschi's adventurous life, spent in many cities from Florence to Rome and then London and Naples, as she was born, grew up and trained as a painter here. She spent two different periods in the city: the first until the autumn of 1612, when she left for Florence after her father Orazio Lomi (Pisa, 1563 – London, 1639) brought charges of rape against Agostino Tassi on her behalf; the second between 1620 and 1627, when she returned surrounded by an extraordinary fame for a woman artist.

The young woman, who lost her mother at the age of twelve, was introduced to painting by her father Orazio, a Pisan painter who taught her to paint using models and guided her towards a naturalism in the style of Caravaggio. She lived in their home-workshop in Via Paolina and then in Via della Croce. She regularly visited churches and oratories, including Santa Maria del Popolo, San Lorenzo in Lucina, Santo Spirito in Sassia, Sant'Onofrio, San Giovanni in Laterano, San Pietro and San Paolo Fuori le Mura. Probably she visited the Borghese lodge at the Quirinal, where her father was working, and was able to attend other worksites that were changing the stylistic trends of the time. The trial papers report that during the 1612 Carnival, a period when the rules of behaviour were less strict, the young woman frequented the house of Cosimo Quorli where she may have seen his collection. Through such means, Artemisia gained an up-to-date knowledge of contemporary art, from Caravaggio to the Cavalier d'Arpino and the Carracci. Moreover, thanks to the engravings belonging to the repertoire of her father's workshop, she was able to study the greats of the Renaissance. She completed her apprenticeship by 1609 and emerged with a particular talent for depicting female nudes, apparent in *Susanna and the Elders* (Pommersfelden, Graf von Schönborn Collection, inv. 191). Collectors and friends of her father, including Agostino Tassi himself, regularly visited the Gentileschi house. Immediately after the infamous trial, on 29 November 1612, Artemisia married Pierantonio Stiattesi and the two moved to Florence. Here she lived for eight years among the stimuli of a sophisticated court, learned to write and developed her own interpretation of naturalism. However, she came fully into her own in Rome. In 1620 she returned to the city and with her husband and daughter Palmira rented a house in Via del Corso and a second in Via della Croce. Artemisia forged relationships with prominent personages and patrons in the Rome of the time, such as Cassiano dal Pozzo and the third Duke of Alcalà, Fernando Afán de Ribera. There is little documentary evidence of her relations with other artists: it is certain only that she knew Simon Vouet, who executed an intense portrait of her (Bergamo, Zaccaria Collection). As concerns others, it can only be presumed that she met Massimo Stanzione, Bartolomeo Manfredi, Spadarino (Giovanni Antonio Galli), Antiveduto Gramatica, Bartolomeo Cavarozzi, Nicolas Tournier and Guercino. Her study of antiquity is apparent in *Susanna and the Elders* (England, Lincolnshire, Burghley House, inv. PIC218), which cites the *Crouching Venus* in the Ludovisi collection; the same painting also shows that she had seen Guercino's *Dawn* in the Casino dell'Aurora and was thus familiar with contemporary art. In 1626 she left Rome, the city in which she had grown up, trained and ultimately become Artemisia the Painter.

BIBLIOGRAPHY: Mary D. Garrard, *Artemisia Gentileschi: The Image of the Female Hero in Italian Baroque Art*. Princeton: Princeton University Press, 1989; *Artemisia*, exhib. cat. (London 2020), ed. by Letizia Treves, London: The National Gallery Company, 2020; Sheila Barker, *Artemisia Gentileschi*. London: Lund Humphries, 2021, 23–83.

Laura Palombaro

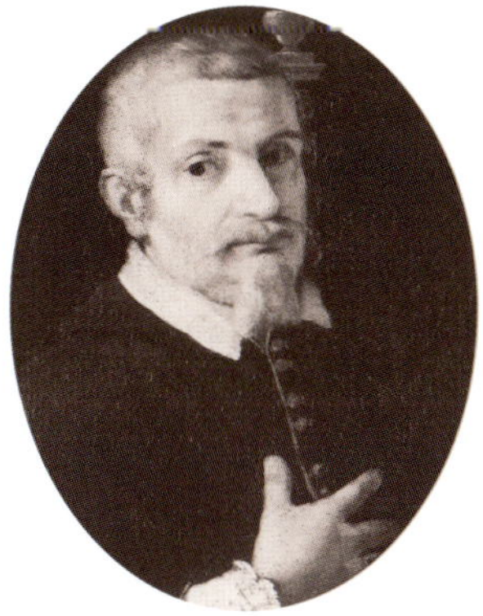

Caterina Ginnasi

(Rome, 1590–1660)

The daughter of Dioniso, a lawyer for the Colonna family, and of Faustina Gottardi, Caterina descended from an illustrious Roman family. She was born in 1590 in the family palace in Via delle Botteghe Oscure, where she lived with her mother, who died in 1646, and her uncle, the powerful Cardinal Domenico Ginnasi. She refused to marry her cousin Francesco so she could dedicate herself to painting. Her uncle placed her under the guidance first of Gaspare Celio and then of Giovanni Lanfranco.

Her first known works are some paintings for the church of Santa Lucia alle Botteghe Oscure, demolished between 1938 and 1941. At this point Caterina's works were moved inside the chapel of Palazzo Ginnasi, where they can still be found today. Giovanni Battista Passeri reports that here the painter depicted a *Martyrdom of St Lucy*, a *Last Supper*, a *Madonna*, a *St Blaise Bishop of Sebaste* and a *St Joseph*.

In 1632, the painter devoted herself to the entire decoration, with canvases and frescoes, of the Ginnasi chapel built by Cardinale Domenico in Velletri cathedral, of which he was the bishop. Removed during repainting works in 1824, the decorative programme comprised an altarpiece with the *Madonna and the Four Patron Saints of Velletri (St Clement, St Gerald, St Pontian and St Eleutherius)*; in the spandrels were the *Four Evangelists*.

In the church of the Angelo Custode in Rome, demolished between 1928 and 1929, she had painted a *Guardian Angel*, maybe in 1637. In 1638, Caterina is documented as a member of the Accademia di San Luca.

The *post-mortem* inventory of her uncle the cardinal lists other paintings by his niece in the palace's painting gallery: *St Catherine of Alexandria*, the Assumption of the Virgin, *The Archangel Michael* and a *Madonna with the Four Patron Saints of Velletri*, probably a copy of the painting for Ginnasi Chapel.

A further two lost oil paintings by the artist are recorded: a *Nativity* and a *Pietà* in the collection of the Pio di Savoia family. To these we should add the *Portrait of Cardinal Ginnasi*, now in the Museo di Roma - Palazzo Braschi (inv. MR 2215).

Caterina died in Rome on 30 November 1660 and was buried in the chapel of San Biagio in the family church, next to her mother and uncle. A marble bust in the Victoria & Albert Museum in London has been identified as a portrait of her, executed in around 1660 by Cosimo Fancelli.

BIBLIOGRAPHY: Franca Trinchieri Camiz, "Virgo-non sterilis... Nuns as Artists in Seventeenth-Century Rome." In *Picturing Women in Renaissance and Baroque Italy*, ed. by Geraldine A. Johnson, Sara F. Matthews Grieco. Cambridge: Cambridge University Press, 1997, 159–64; Olga Melasecchi, s.v. "Ginnasi, Caterina." In *Dizionario biografico degli Italiani*. Vol. 55. Rome: Istituto della Enciclopedia Italiana, 2002, 21–3.

Consuelo Lollobrigida

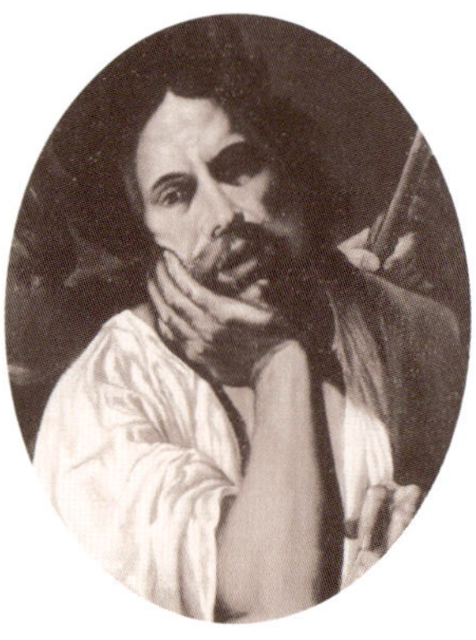

Giustiniana Guidotti Borghesi

(Rome, 1600?–1634)

In his biography of Paolo Guidotti called il Cavalier Borghese (*c.* 1560–1629), Giovanni Baglione makes reference to "his only daughter, whom he is educating with all possible diligence in all the virtues, both feminine and masculine". This is almost certainly an allusion to his daughter Giustiniana, probably born in around 1600 as we can deduce from the certificate of her confirmation in 1607, which also tells us that she lived in the parish of Santa Maria in Trastevere. The identification of her name in the "List of New Members of the Academy elected on 3 April 1633" in the Archive of the Accademia di San Luca (of dubious authenticity given the presence of some later additions) suggests that at this date Giustiniana had amply demonstrated her abilities as a painter. Proof of this is the signed painting in which she depicts the *Allegory of Poetry and Music* (now in the Koelliker collection), whose style suggests an artistic training in her home-workshop. It is highly likely that she lived with her family between the Trastevere and Borgo districts, at least until 1629, when her father (buried at Santa Maria in Traspontina) named her his sole heir. Her presence in other lists of the Accademia di San Luca dated 1651 and 1655 has always suggested that she was still alive then while, at the same time, the absence of her name from the parish registers for those years suggested a move to Lucca, her father's hometown. Despite this, the discovery of her will has made it possible to date her premature death to around 14 February 1634. Nonetheless, the hypothesis that she spent some time in Lucca remains valid: during the 18th century, the local scholar Giovanni Sardini, later echoed by Giacomo Cerù, writes that the painter "made no little progress, as demonstrated in past times by her small painting in the Cathedral in the Chapel of the Volto Sacro; it has been impossible for me to discover any trace of other paintings that she executed". The work mentioned can be identified as the *Madonna and Child with Saints*, now in the cathedral museum and on the back of whose frame we read "Mrs Giustiniana Borghesi Guidotti". The fact that this is clearly an *ex voto* painting (inscription on the bottom left) has led scholars to assume that it was a gift from Giustiniana of a painting by her father. In any case, Sardini's note clearly indicates that a painting by her was kept in the chapel of the Volto Santo.

BIBLIOGRAPHY: Michele Nicolaci, "Aggiornamenti e nuove proposte per Paolo Borghese Guidotti tra Roma e Lucca." In *Artisti e committenti lucchesi del Seicento a Roma*, conference proceedings (Rome 2016), ed. by Stefan Albl, Sybille Ebert-Schifferer, Michele Nicolaci. Milan: Officina Libraria, 2018, 45–7.

Ilaria Arcangeli

Camilla Guiscardi (Gandolfi), *Genoese Women Offering Their Jewellery for the Crusade Against the Moors*, 1840. Turin, Musei Reali, Palazzo Reale (detail).

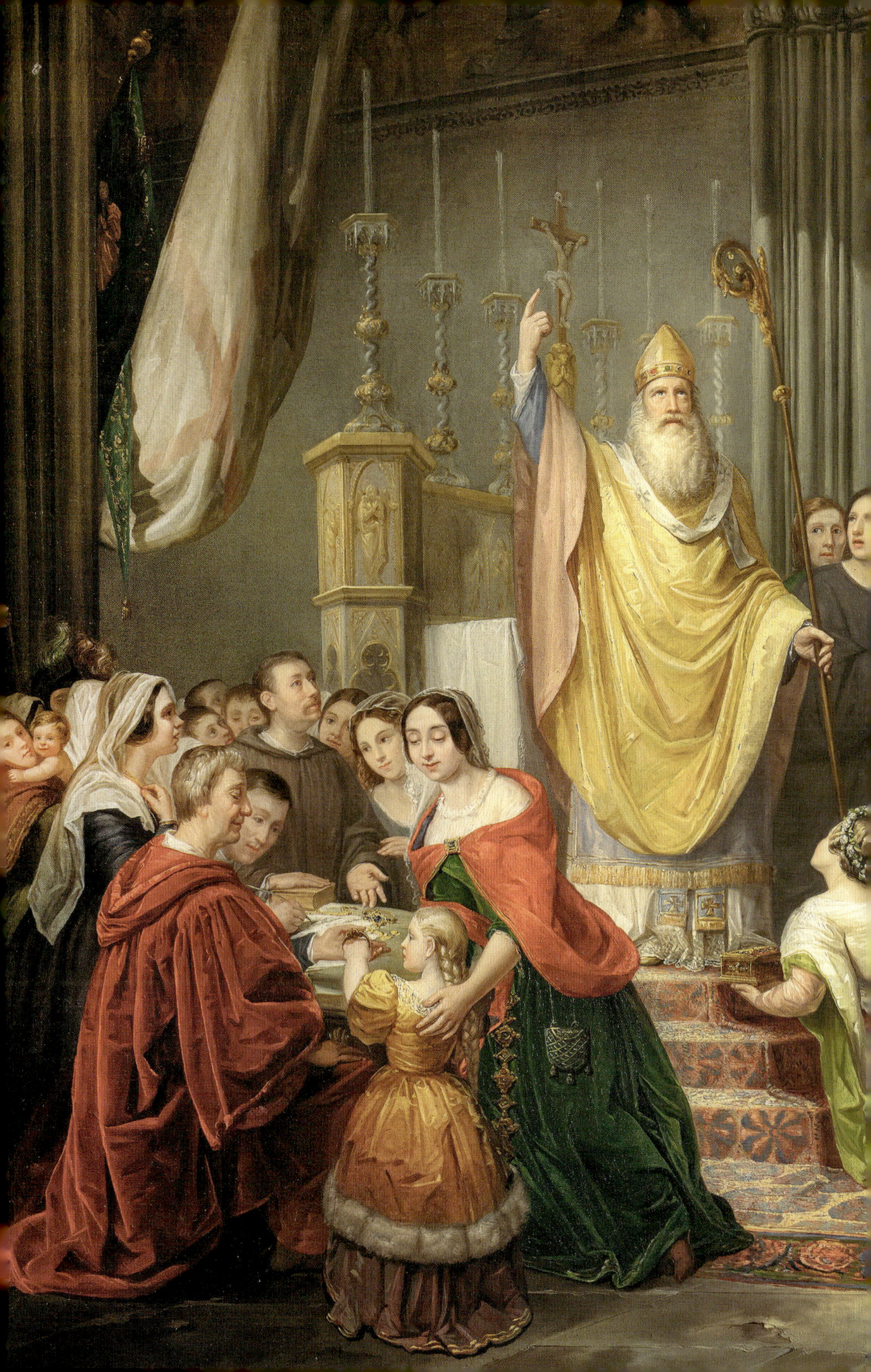

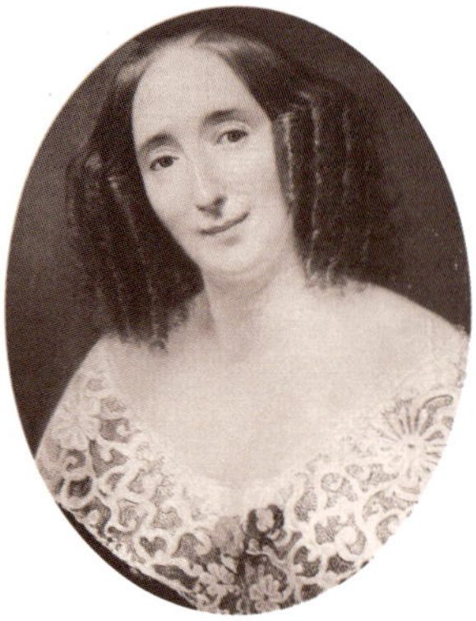

Camilla Guiscardi (Gandolfi)

(Genoa, 1806 – Florence, 1893)

The painter was born in 1806 in Genoa, where for the first three years of her life she was registered as Camilla Guasconi, only taking the last name Guiscardi when she was officially recognized by her biological father in 1809. She moved to Milan at an early age, studying first at the Collegio Viale, and then "moving intrepidly to the study of painting" with Ernesta Legnani. The first phase of her production is linked to practice pieces, copying the masterpieces in the Accademia di Brera. She participated in almost all the Milanese exhibitions from 1821 to 1840, and then continued her work in Turin, where she improved thanks to the teachings of Pelagio Palagi (1775–1860). In around 1834, she married the lawyer Emanuele Gandolfi, and the couple moved to Turin where their son Riccardo, who became a renowned music critic, was born in 1839. The painter's biographer Federigo Alizeri recalls that Camilla "perfected her style several times in Rome and several times in Florence", where she moved in 1844 to study with Giuseppe Bezzuoli. Few documentary traces survive of her time in Rome, but her election to the Congregazione dei Virtuosi al Pantheon, again in 1844 on the proposal of Francesco Podesti, and her life spent between Turin and Florence until her death on 9 February 1893, lead us to believe that the painter travelled to Rome several times between 1834 and 1838. There she frequented the painter from Ancona, who nominated her as soon he became president of the Virtuosi in 1844. From 1842, after becoming honorary painter to King Charles Albert of Savoy, she presented her works at the Promotrice di Torino exhibitions for a decade. In 1852 she returned to Genoa, where she was elected member of the Accademia Ligustica. Her prolific production includes portraits, miniatures and copies after contemporary paintings (a famous example is the *Last Farewell of Juliet and Romeo* by Francesco Hayez). Particularly noteworthy are her history paintings on original subjects, including the scenes for the Galleria del Daniel in Turin's Palazzo Reale, and above all the two monumental canvases with *The Women of Genoa Offer Their Jewels for the Crusade Against the Moors* (1840, Turin, Palazzo Reale, inv. 7584) and *Innocent IV Flees from Frederick II and is Received in Genoa by the Podestà* (1849, Agliè, Castello Ducale). Her works as a printmaker are also fine, chief among them the album *Ritratti delle donne italiane viventi che si distinguono nelle scienze nelle lettere e nelle arti belle* (1838, Milan, Vassalli).

BIBLIOGRAPHY: M.C. Gozzoli, in *Cultura figurativa e architettonica negli Stati del Re di Sardegna (1773–1861)*, exhib. cat. (Turin 1980), ed. by Enrico Castelnuovo, Marco Rosci, 3 vols. Turin: Regione Piemonte–Provincia di Torino, 1980, 1:401, nos. 374–75; 3:1450-51; F. Mazzocca, *ibid.*, 1:504, no. 504; A.L. Genovese, in *La collezione della Pontificia Insigne Accademia di Belle Arti e Lettere dei Virtuosi al Pantheon. Dipinti e sculture*, ed. by Vitaliano Tiberia, Adriana Capriotti, Paolo Castellani. Rome: Scripta Manent, 2016, 216–17.

Vanda Lisanti

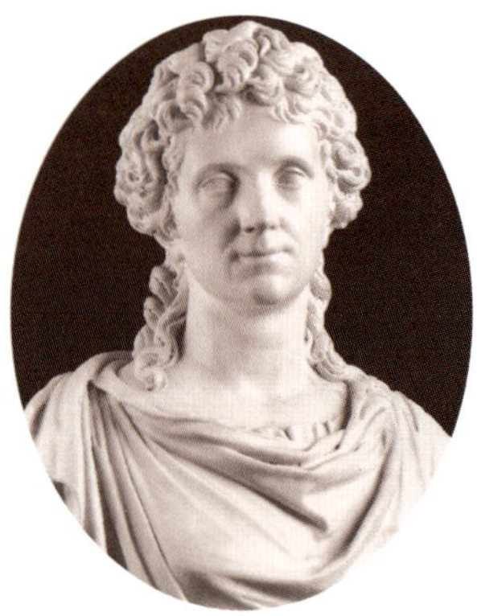

Angelika Kauffmann

(Chur, Grisons, 1741 – Rome, 1807)

Angelica Kauffman was one of the most celebrated and prolific women artists of her time. Her extraordinary career unfolded prevalently in Rome, where she lived for over twenty-five years.

Kauffmann was trained in the context of Lombard and Venetian art under the guidance of her father, a modest painter devoted particularly to nurturing the precocious talents of his daughter. In addition to painting, she studied literature and philosophy, and learned languages, music and singing. Already determined to become a painter, she first lived in Rome between 1763 and 1765. Here she made some important friends: in addition to Johann Joachim Winckelmann, she frequented artists such as Gavin Hamilton, Pompeo Batoni and Giovanni Battista Piranesi. She practiced figure composition by studying ancient sculpture and nude drawings, and executed historical and allegorical paintings such as *Hope*, given to the Accademia di San Luca on the occasion of her admission in 1765 (inv. 286). She also painted the portraits of numerous members of Roman cosmopolitan society. Her portrait of the Shakespearean actor *David Garrick* (1764, Stamford, Burghley House Collection, inv. PIC176), executed during a stay in Naples and displayed at the Free Society, marked her first success in London, amply confirmed during her years in the English city (1766–1781). In 1782 she was back in Rome. She settled in the Stefanoni house in Via Felice, formerly the residence of many illustrious artists, and her studio and elegant salons soon became some of the greatest attractions of the Roman Grand Tour.

During this period, she executed a number of her most important works, including the *Self-Portrait with the Bust of Minerva* (1780, Chur, Bündner Kunstmuseum, inv. 321.000.1945) and *Cornelia Mother of the Gracchi* (1785, Richmond, Virginia Museum of Fine Arts, inv. 75-22). Sacred subjects, alongside historical and literary topics, formed a central part of the painter's late production, culminating in the prestigious commission for the *Education of the Virgin*, intended for the sanctuary of Loreto (1790–1791). She died in Rome in 1807, surrounded by glory and admiration. During her funeral service, attended by the members of the Accademia di San Luca and organized by Antonio Canova, "amidst an immense crowd" the painter's body was taken to the church of Sant'Andrea delle Fratte. Here, in the vicinity of her own paintings, almost as if to restore her to life, the artist's "right hand (which a dear friend had had moulded in plaster) was positioned once again as if it held a brush", as Giovanni Gherardo De Rossi wrote in 1810.

BIBLIOGRAPHY: *Angelika Kauffmann 1741–1807. Retrospektive*, exhib. cat. (Düsseldorf-Munich-Chur 1998–99), ed. by Bettina Baumgärtel. Düsseldorf: Ostfildern, 1998 ; Wendy Wassyng Roworth, "'The Residence of the Arts': Angelica Kauffman's Place in Rome." In *Italy's Eighteenth Century: Gender and Culture in the Age of the Grand Tour*, ed. by Paula Findlen, Wendy Wassyng Roworth, Catherine M. Sama, Stanford: Stanford University Press, 2009, 151–71.

Jessica Calipari

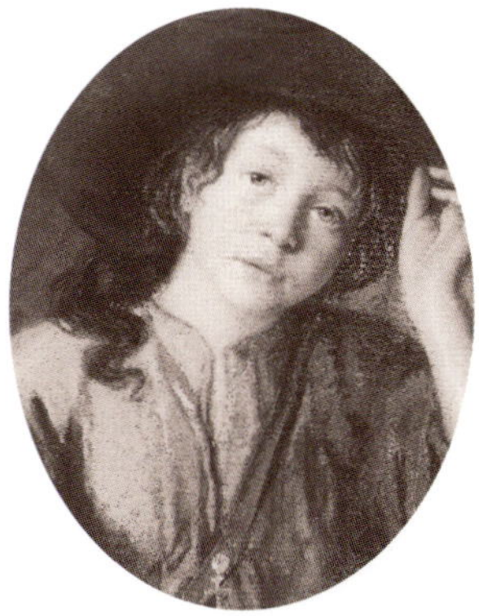

Hortense Lescot (Haudebourt)

(Paris, 1784–1845)

After losing her father in 1786, Hortense Viel studied painting from an early age with Guillaume Guillon-Lethière (1760–1832), a friend of her mother. During adolescence, she took her stepfather's the last name and began her career under the name of Hortense Lescot.

A young star of contradance under the French Directory, she was introduced into the luxurious and unconventional society of the period following the Thermidorian Reaction. Alongside the celebrities Joséphine de Beauharnais (1763–1814), Madame Tallien (Thérésia Cabarrus, 1773–1835) and Madame Hamelin (Jeanne Geneviève Fortunée Lormier-Lagrave, 1776–1851), she shone at Parisian public dances. However, it was her talent as a painter that earned her the greatest renown.

Her career as a painter began when she accompanied Guillaume Guillon-Lethière, of whom she was a student, to Italy in 1807 after he was appointed director of the Académie de France à Rome. The city and its inhabitants turned out to be a source of inspiration for the young artist. At the sight of a group of pipers in front of a Madonna, she decided to represent the scene in a painting: the depiction of the ordinary people of Rome thus became her fa-

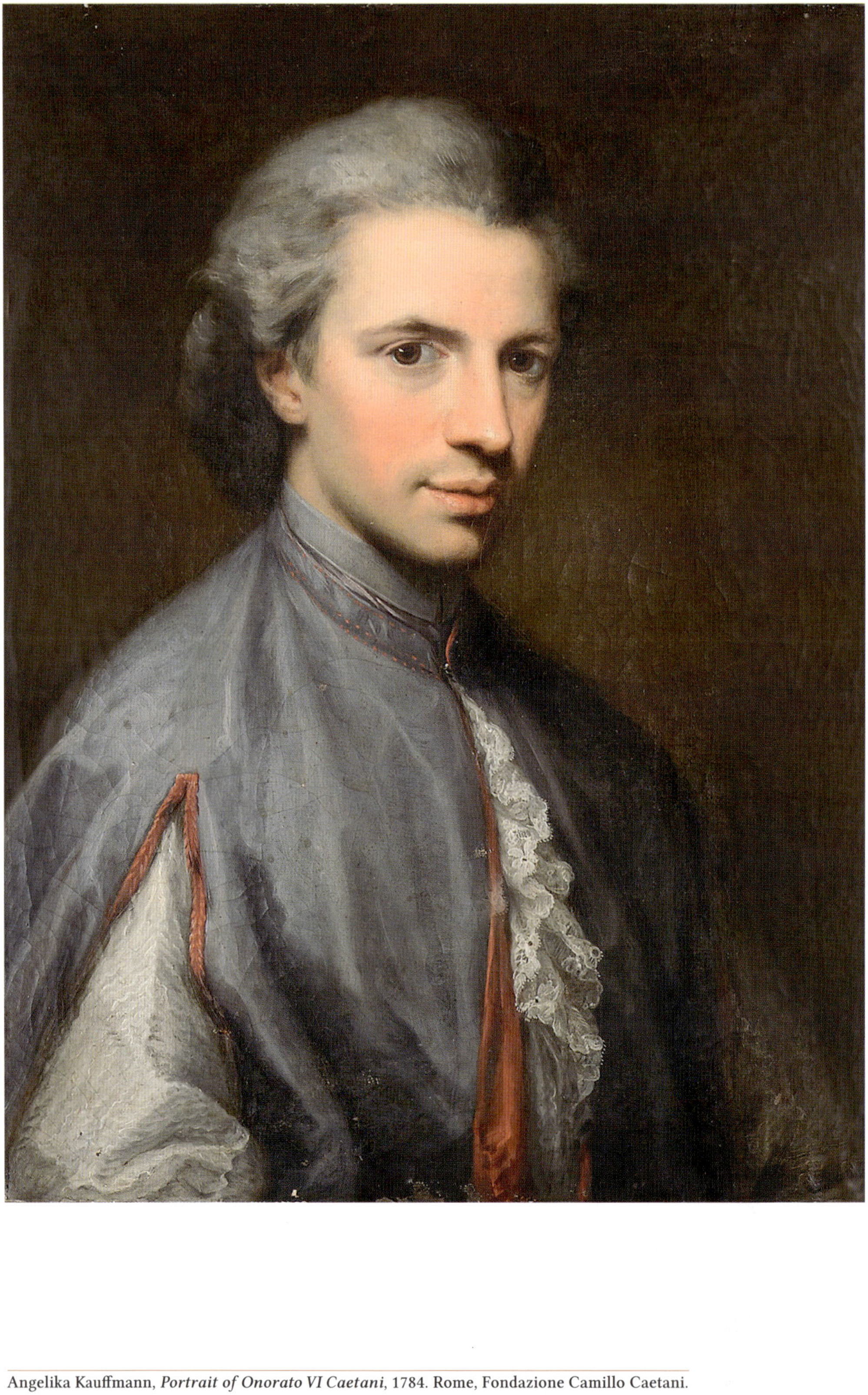

Angelika Kauffmann, *Portrait of Onorato VI Caetani*, 1784. Rome, Fondazione Camillo Caetani.

Hortense Lescot (Haudebourt), *The Little Beggar*, 1810. Private Collection.

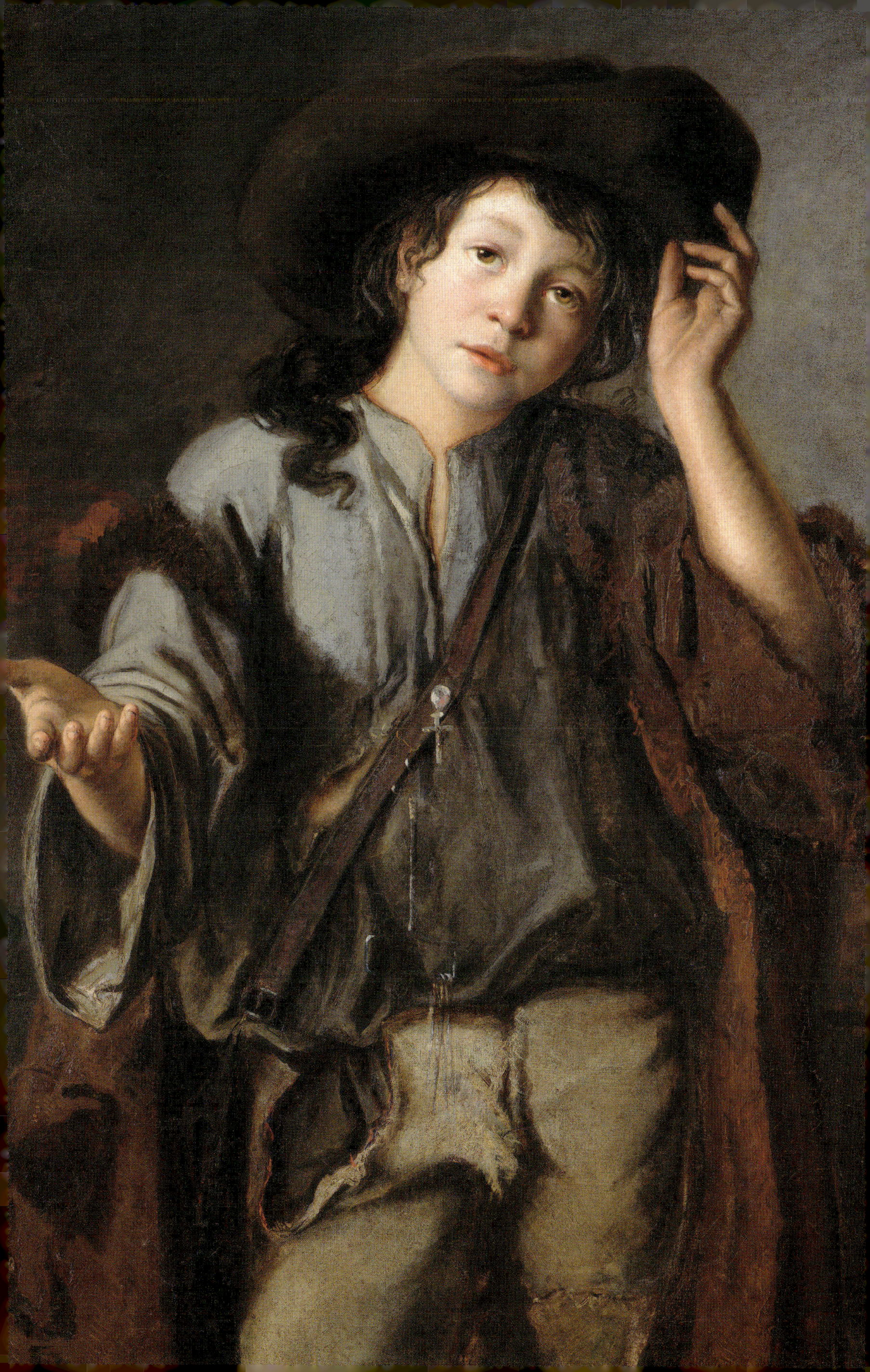

voured genre. During her long career, lasting over thirty years, Hortense Lescot, who became Haudebourt-Lescot following her marriage in 1820 to the architect Louis-Pierre Haudebourt (1788–1849), continued to focus on the representation of Italian folk scenes alongside history painting. In late 1809, she made her debut at the exhibition of international artists organized at the Palazzo Senatorio by the Napoleonic Council under the direction of General François de Miollis. She displayed a "beggar wrapped in his cloak" (today in Paris, Musée Carnavalet, inv. P765) together with other portraits of members of the Napoleonic circle and three genre scenes. Among the works executed on this occasion, many of which were also presented at the *Salon* of the following year (like the *Little Beggar*, that garnered considerable critical acclaim), was the portrait of the architect Pierre-Adrien Pâris, submitted by the artist herself to the Accademia di San Luca on her admission and now in the Musée des Beaux-Arts et d'Archéologie of Besançon (inv. 876.4.2).

On returning to France in 1814, Hortense received numerous official honours. Appointed painter to the Duchess of Berry (Marie-Caroline of Bourbon, 1798–1870) in 1816, her first masterpieces (*Kissing the Feet of the Statue of St Peter in St. Peter's, Rome*, 1812, Musée national du château de Fontainebleau, inv. 5284; *The Confirmation Celebrated by a Greek Bishop in the Basilica of St. Agnes Outside the Walls*, 1814, Musée de Rouen, inv. D.1874.3) were purchased by the French state and the artist received her first royal commission for Fontainebleau (*Diane de Poitier*, 1819, Musée national du Château de Fontainebleau, inv. 5282). At the Salon, her work was awarded two first-class medals in 1819 and 1827.

Under the July Monarchy, Hortense Lescot Haudebourt received no less than eleven commissions for the Musée Historique de Versailles. When the museum opened, the painter was one of only two women artists invited to the royal banquet; the second was Herminie Déhérain (1798–1839), her student and friend.

In the final years of her life, she devoted herself almost exclusively to teaching girls to paint. Alongside other renowned painters, such as Joséphine Sarazin de Belmont (1790–1871) and Lizinka de Mirbel (1796–1849), she participated in the innovative but short-lived project between 1837 and 1840, to establish an École des Beaux-Arts pour les femmes.

BIBLIOGRAPHY: Melissa Hyde, "«Peinte par elle-même?» Femmes artistes, professeures et étudiantes d'Anguissola à Haudebourt-Lescot." In *Autoportraits, autofictions de femmes à l'époque moderne*, ed. by Caroline Trotot. Paris: Garnier, 2018, 221–53; Paul Menoux, "Le fameux salon d'Hortense Haudebourt-Lescot." *Dossier de l'art*, nos. 286 (2021), 20–1.

Paul Menoux

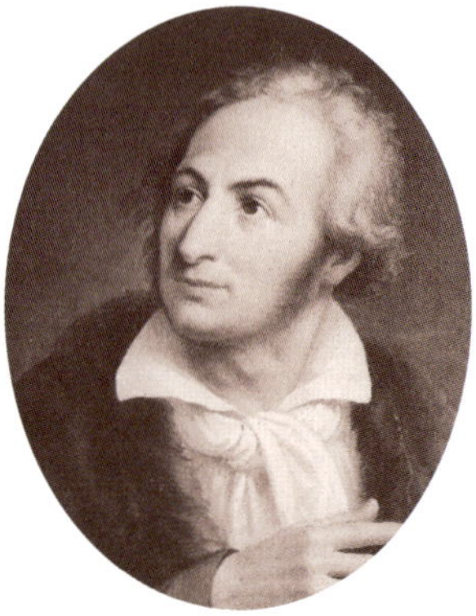

Luisa Martignoni Bigioli
(Rome, 1831–1890)

The daughter of Giuseppe Martignoni and of Caterina Moretti, Luisa Martignoni took the last name of her stepfather Filippo Bigioli when her mother married her second husband, a painter originally from San Severino Marche, at the parish church of Sant'Andrea delle Fratte. Thanks to him, Luisa devoted herself to art, specializing in portraits and figure paintings at her Rome studio in Via Sistina no. 79.

The artist is known for her execution of a portrait of the poet Vincenzo Monti (Rome, Museo di Roma, inv. Dep. Arch. 17), which the *Giornale arcadico di scienze, lettere ed arti* (1852) describes as follows in an article on the poet: "the Roman damsel Luisa Bigioli had only to apprehend the universal desire for her to portray Vincenzo Monti with such mastery as to reveal herself a worthy daughter to Professor Filippo. Who could fail to identify in these majestic forms the greatest man of his time, as Giordani called him?".

In 1853, Luisa Bigioli won the Gregoriano competition organized by the Congregazione dei Virtuosi al Pantheon for her interpretation of the theme: *Ahasuerus King of Persia Surprises Haman Supplicating Queen Esther*. The painting won over the jury for "its simple and clear contents and composition, perfectly in keeping with the programme [...]" (Rome, Pontificia Accademia dei Virtuosi al Pantheon Archive, *Concorsi*, aa. 1838–1920). In accordance with the competition regulations, the work entered the collections of the Virtuosi, but the artist had to wait two years before receiving her prize: the Archiginnasio, or University of Rome La Sapienza, where the ceremony was to be held, did not admit women at this time. It was only thanks to the diplomatic efforts of the president in perpetuity, Giuseppe de Fabris, that on 2 February 1854 Bigioli obtained the recognition she deserved. On 13 June 1858, again on the proposal of de Fabris, Luisa was admitted as a member of the society; a few months later she gave the congregation a portrait of Giovanni Domenico Navone (Rome, Pontificia Accademia dei Virtuosi al Pantheon, inv. 115).

The painter is mentioned critically in an article of 29 October 1855 in the *Annales archéologiques*, for her execution of a *Mary Magdalene* for an *Esposizione di industria e arte* held periodically in Rome: "A harsh penance would have been imposed on Giuseppe Lazzarini, from Carrara, and on Luisa Bigioli, from Rome, had one insisted that their St Sebastian and St Mary Magdalene be clothed".

In 1857, she participated in the customary Rome exhibition of the Società degli amatori e cultori delle belle arti with a painting entitled *The Conception*.

Bigioli died in destitution on 10 April 1890, at the age of 58, in her house in Via San Basilio no. 75. The painter was buried on 13 April 1890 and her remains were later transferred to the communal ossuary in the Verano cemetery.

BIBLIOGRAPHY: Anna Lisa Genovese, "La premiazione nei concorsi gregoriani (1838-1874) delle pittrici Amalia de Angelis, Erminia Pompili e Luisa Bigioli." In *Annali della Pontificia Insigne Accademia di Belle Arti e Lettere dei Virtuosi al Pantheon* 14 (2014), 368, 376–80; Ead., "Luisa Bigioli." In *La collezione della Pontificia Insigne Accademia di Belle Arti e Lettere dei Virtuosi al Pantheon. Dipinti e sculture*, ed. by Vitaliano Tiberia, Adriana Capriotti, Paolo Castellani. Rome: Scripta Manent, 2016, 232–35.

Alice Militello

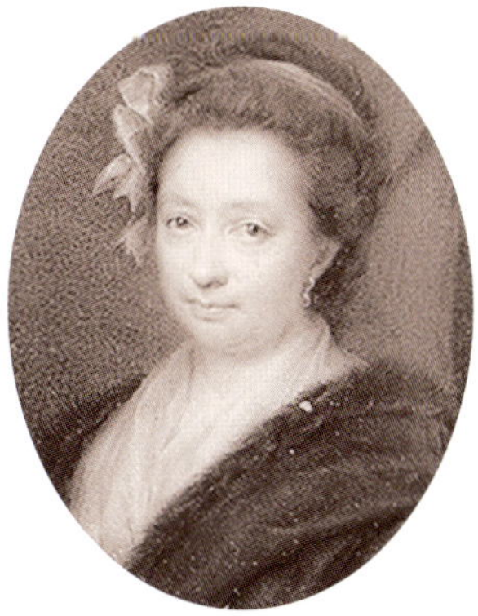

Therese Concordia Mengs (von Maron)

(Ústí nad Labem, 1725 – Rome, 1806)

Therese was the daughter of Ismael Mengs (1691/1692–1764), court painter to the Elector of Saxony and King of Poland Augustus III. She received her initial training alongside her siblings, Anton Raphael (1728–1779) and Julie Charlotte (1730–after 1806), at the "Painting Academy", as Giovanni Lodovico Bianconi defined it, established by her strict father within their home.

Though known primarily for her exquisite miniatures, Mengs began her career as a pastellist and also practiced painting on enamel. In 1741, she travelled to Rome with her family for the first time and stayed for three years. On her return to Dresden, she was appointed cabinet painter to the Saxon court in October 1745, with an annual pension of 300 talers. Her pastels, like those of her brother and sister, entered the royal collection and were displayed in the so-called "Cabinet of Rosalba". This room on the first floor of the Gemäldegalerie displayed pastels by well-known artists in addition to various works by Rosalba Carriera. The protection of the sovereign allowed the Mengs family to return to Rome in 1747. From 1752, Therese lived permanently in the Eternal City. Here she continued to work alongside her brother; after the latter's departure for Spain, she continued her career independently. In 1765 she married the painter Anton von Maron (Vienna, 1733 – Rome, 1808) and the following year was appointed member of the Accademia di San Luca. In addition to being an esteemed and in-demand painter, Mengs was also a successful teacher. Many women artists, including her niece Anna Maria, undertook their specialist training in small-format painting at her school. She worked with the "same diligence, precision and soft touch", as we read in an issue of *Diario ordinario* in 1806, as in her youth until a month before her death on 10 October 1806. The Roman press, which took a special interest in the painter's professional life, records numerous works made during her career. Many of these were sent to Russia to the court of Catherine II, her great admirer and client for over twenty-five years. Of this vast production, consisting mainly of miniatures drawn from famous masterpieces, few works are known today. They include the copies of Correggio's *Day* and *Night* in the Gemäldegalerie in Dresden (inv. Gal. Nr M 63, Gal. Nr. M 64) together with her famous self-portrait, a portrait of her sister (inv. Gal. Nr. P 179, Gal. Nr. P 178) and a drawing with *St John the Baptist* (Dresden, Kupferstich-Kabinett, inv. C 7698).

BIBLIOGRAPHY: Olivier Michel, "Peintres autrichiens à Rome dans la seconde moitié du XVIIIe siècle." In *Vivre et peindre à Rome au XVIIIe siècle.* Rome: École française de Rome, 1996, 391–402; Steffi Roettgen, *Anton Raphael Mengs 1728-1779. Leben und Wirke.* Munich: Hirmer, 2003, 70–2, 79, 220, 285, 464–66, 491, 507, 512, 515, 517, 556, 596; Anna Sexton, "Pastellmalerei in Dresden. Von Rosalba Carriera bis Theresa Concordia Mengs." In *Aus dem Schatten. Künstlerinnen vom 16. bis zum 18. Jahrhundert*, exhib. cat. (Dresden 2023), ed. by Stephan Koja, Iris Yvonne Wagner, Dresden: Sandstein, 2023, 99–103.

Jessica Calipari

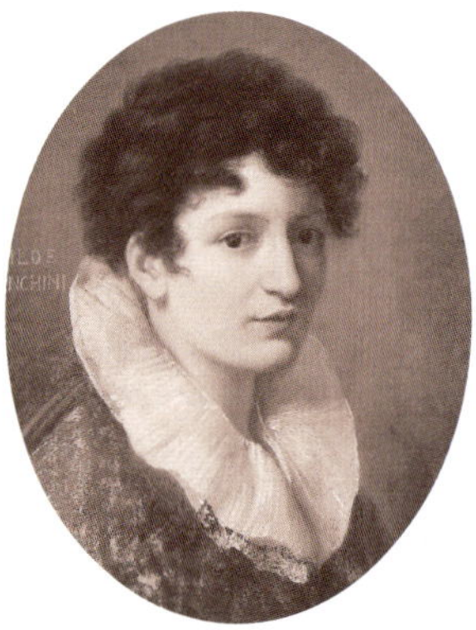

Matilde Meoni (Malenchini)

(Leghorn, 1779 – Fiesole, 1858)

Matilde Meoni, the daughter of Luigi Meoni and of Francesca Ferrandi, married the Livornese Vincenzo Francesco Malenchini in 1796. From 1807 she attended the Accademia di Belle Arti of Florence under the guidance of the Neoclassical painter Pietro Benvenuti (Arezzo, 1796 – Florence, 1817). Between 1807 and 1812 numerous requests to the Gallerie degli Uffizi for permission to make copies are recorded in the painter's name; these mainly concern works of the 17th century (Peter Paul Rubens, Guido Reni and Flemish artists). In 1809 she participated in the *Mostra internazionale* at the Capitoline with another six women artists (Bianca Boni, Maria Cecconi, Hortense Lescot, Rosa Mezzera, Saveria De Simoni), displaying seven portraits of famous men. In 1811 she was awarded a four-year scholarship by the Grand Ducal court that allowed her to continue her studies in Rome. Among her greatest admirers were Antonio Canova and the French general and collector Sextius Alexandre François de Miollis, who provided her with a studio in the convent of Trinità dei Monti at the Académie de France, where she lived between 1814 and 1816. Coming into contact with the circle of international artists from France and the Netherlands, she gradually acquired a predilection for genre painting and interiors in the manner of François Marius Granet. On 20 August 1815 she was proclaimed member of the Accademia di San Luca with the support of Andrea Pozzi, Filippo Agricola and Vincenzo Camuccini. Her painting *A Holy Thursday Service in the Sistine Chapel* (now in a private collection) dates to between 1816 and 1818; it was commissioned from her by Maria Luisa of Spain and earned her the praise of king Carlos IV of Spain and of "all intelligent people" (as we read in an issue of the *Gazzetta di Firenze* in 1818). In 1821 she was appointed honorary professor of the Accademia di Belle Arti of Florence. From 1823 she travelled between Rome, Florence, Leghorn, Paris and Brussels. On 4 June 1834 she was elected member of the Congregazione dei Virtuosi al Pantheon and in 1844 was awarded a life-time pension by the Grand Duchy of Tuscany. She died in Fiesole on 8 September 1858.

BIBLIOGRAPHY: Marijcke Schillings, "Malenchini-Meoni, Maria Matilde, genoemd Matilde, Toscaanse schilderes en geliefde van Louis de Potter." In *Nationaal Biografisch Woordenboek*, ed. by W. Waterschoot, Hans Rombaut 21 (2014), 697–709; Anna Lisa Genovese, "DIARIO 1800–1834." In Vitaliano Tiberia, *La Congregazione dei Virtuosi al Pantheon da Pio VII a Pio IX.* Galatina: Congedo, 2015, 334

Michela D'Agostino

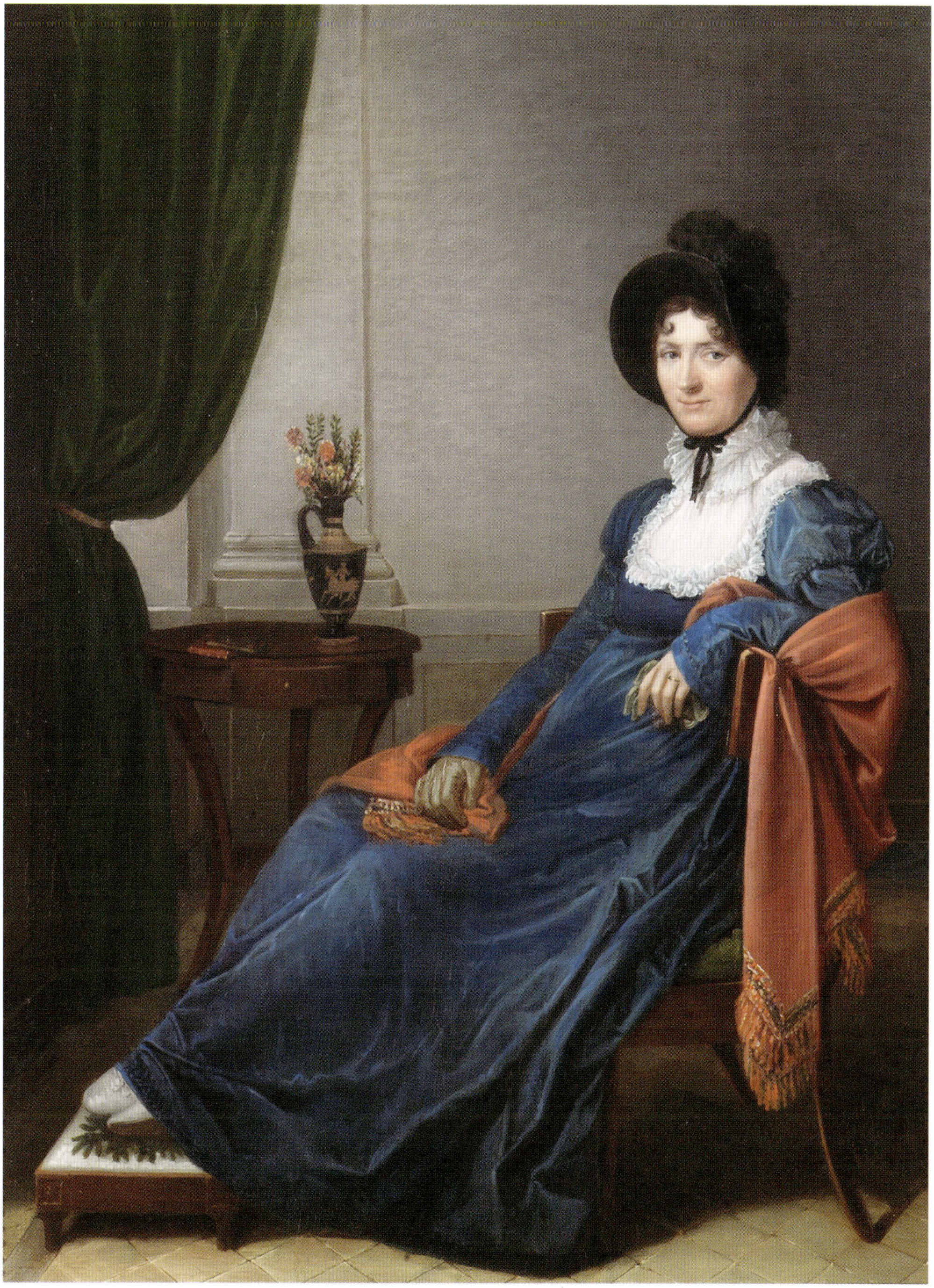

Matilde Meoni (Malenchini), *Portrait of Madame Le Bon*, 1813. Private Collection.

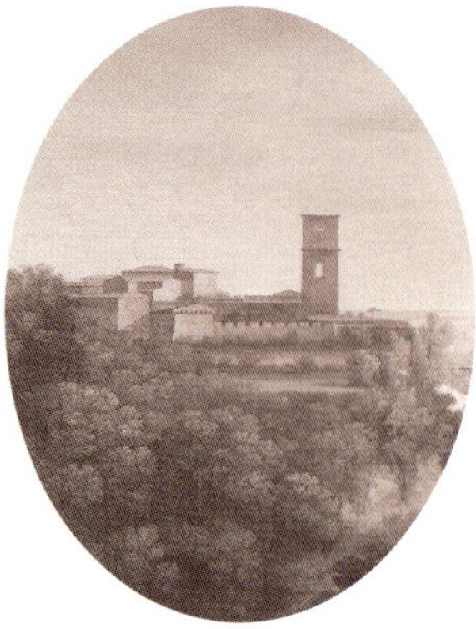

Rosa Mezzera

(Bergamo, *c.* 1780 – Rome, 1826)

Rosa Mezzera, the first woman student at the Accademia di Brera and the first to receive a scholarship to study in Rome, where she was active from 1802, is listed by the sources among the Lombard pioneers of landscape painting. Few of the artist's works survive and these are in the Accademia di Brera (inv. 1980-335, 1980-336, 1980-337, 1980-338, 1980-339, reg. 1943, 16). Equally scanty is the information on her career, spent almost entirely in Rome. From the correspondence of her protector Pietro Verri, we learn that Mezzera supported her family in Bergamo financially with her work as a painter. At the height of the Napoleonic period her classicizing style was much appreciated in the Roman art world, as demonstrated by her admission to the Accademia di San Luca in 1808, her participation in the exhibition held on the Capitoline the following year and the information available on her network of buyers and protectors, which included prominent figures like Antonio Canova and the Duchess of Sora, Maddalena Odescalchi.

Very little is known about the period after 1812, the year in which Rosa Mezzera made a brief visit to Bergamo after enjoying a long period as a scholarship recipient. She returned to Rome without financial support, as we are informed by Giuseppe Tambroni in the *Cenno intorno allo stato attuale delle belle arti in Roma* of 1814, which describes her as a "talented woman artist". Some information on Mezzera is also provided by the list of artists working in Rome drawn up in 1824 by Enrico Keller, who mentions her studio, describes her as a "professor at the Accademia di San Luca" and adds that "she gives drawing lessons". Melchiorre Missirini praises her in his *Necrologio* and mentions her students, while the *Diario di Roma*, a year after her death, notes that many of her drawings remained on display in her studio on the top floor apartment at Via Felice no. 126.

BIBLIOGRAPHY: Margherita Zanardi Ricci, "Rosa Mezzera." In *I pittori bergamaschi dell'Ottocento*. Vol. 1. *Il primo Romanticismo. L'Accademia*, ed. by Gian Alberto Dell'Acqua. Bergamo: Bolis, 1993, 232–46; Chiara Nenci, "Rosa Mezzera." In *La Sala dei Paesaggi 1817–1822*, exhib. cat. (Milan 2009), ed. by Isabella Marelli. Milan: Mondadori Electa, 2009, 98–9.

Jessica Calipari

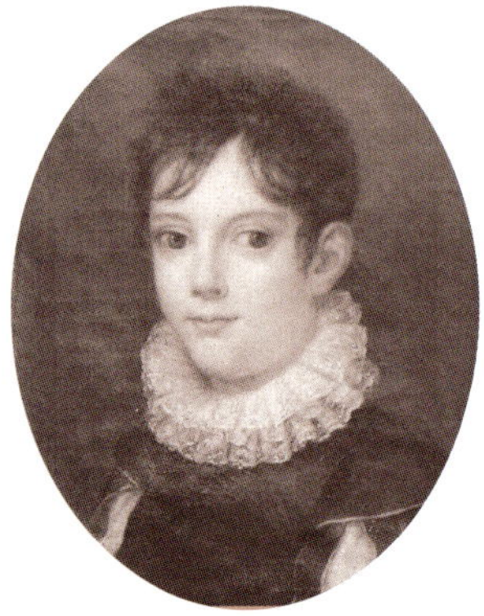

Bianca Milesi (Mojon)

(Milan, 1790 – Paris, 1849)

Included by Carlo Porta among the stars of Milanese art, Bianca Milesi was a writer, artist and patriot. The daughter of the celebrated *salonnière* Elena Viscontini, she began her artistic apprenticeship in Milan with Andrea Appiani before moving to Rome in 1810. Initially accompanied by her mother, who returned to Milan after a year, Milesi moved into a studio near San Vitale, determined to continue her training in the Eternal City. From 1812 she shared accomodation with the German painter Sophie Reinhard. At this time, supported by her older colleague, she dedicated herself tirelessly to the "Divine Art of Painting" (Letter of 26 April 1813 sent from Rome to the physicist Giambattista Venturi) and between 1811 and 1813 joined in group excursions with other artists, travelling as far afield as Campania.

Despite the intensity of this formative period, few traces of Milesi's Roman production have emerged. In addition to a portrait of Prince Caetani as a boy, seventeen drawings are known, contained in the little volume of *Amori* (1758) by Ludovico Savioli, given to the Moldavian poet Gheorghe Asachi (Central Library of Drobeta-Turnu Severin). By contrast, her relations with artists and intellectuals are well-documented. Her friends included Giovanni Gherardo De Rossi, Giuseppe Tambroni, Antonio Canova, Joseph Anton Koch and Francesco Hayez. The latter, also in Rome to attend the Accademia del Regno Italico at Palazzo Venezia, recalls her in his memoirs as a fellow student. After returning to Milan in 1815, Bianca Milesi drew on her Roman apprenticeship to continue her artistic career. An assiduous presence at the Brera exhibitions, she made her final appearance here in 1821 with eight oil portraits that were favourably reviewed by the local press. In the same year, suspected of direct involvement in the Milan uprisings, she began a period of travel: after a stay in Genoa – where support for Mazzini was particularly strong – and a brief return to Milan, she lived in Paris, London (where she displayed at the Royal Academy), the Netherlands, Belgium and Switzerland. In 1825, having returned to Genoa, Milesi married the doctor Benedetto Mojon. During these years, she continued to pursue her political activism and became increasingly interested in teaching, a discipline to which she devoted numerous writings. She wrote from Turin to her friend Fulvia Jacopetti Verri in 1833 that she preferred visiting kindergartens "in which we directly advance the social machinery" over museums and galleries. In 1833 she moved with her family to Paris, where she died in 1849, after contracting cholera while nursing the sick.

BIBLIOGRAPHY: Arianna Arisi Rota, s.v. "Milesi, Bianca." In *Dizionario biografico degli Italiani.* Vol. 74. Rome: Istituto della Enciclopedia Italiana, 2010, 477–80; Federico Piscopo, *Bianca Milesi. Arte e patria nella Milano risorgimentale.* Crespano di Pieve del Grappa: Tipografia Melchiori, 2020.

Jessica Calipari

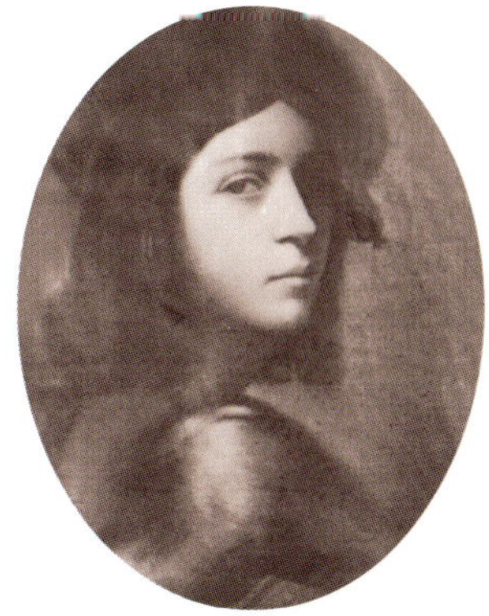

Anna Muschi (Teerlink)

(Castel del Piano, Siena, 1800 – Rome, 1885)

The daughter of Ottavio, originally from Bigorio in the Lugano area of the Canton of Ticino, and of Luisa Arrighi, Anna Muschi was born into a prominent family in a small town on the slopes of Mount Amiata. She learned the first rudiments of art from her father, who had in his turn been a student of Gioacchino Sorbelli (known from 1742 to 1784), a competent local painter who had also worked for some time in Rome. To this city Anna Muschi moved at an early age "to learn the art of painting" (Castel del Piano, Archivio Diocesano di Montalcino, folder 96, Arcipretura e Benefizi). She became an excellent copyist and portraitist, to the extent that in 1836 the Pontificia Accademia di Belle Arti in Bologna awarded her a diploma for these artistic talents.

The Dutch painter, sculptor and architect Johan Philip Koelman (1818–1893) also recollects her as being fond of spending "much of her time in the Vatican, [and] no one surpassed her in copying" (as Maria Luisa Trebiliani wrote).

The Corsini Archive holds a 19th century register recording the requests made by artists to be "allowed to copy in the Gallery, which paintings and when". Anna Muschi is a constant presence between 1841 and 1853, and it is during this period that she executed the copy of the *Violinist*, by Sebastiano del Piombo. Among the painter's other copies, the sources mention three versions of the *Madonna and Child* by Bartolomé Esteban Murillo, including an oil on canvas (cm 240 × 120) given in 1838 by the artist and her husband Abraham Teerlink to the church of the Madonna delle Grazie in Castel del Piano; two versions of Guido Reni's *Herodias*; six *Madonnas* after Carlo Dolci; two *Ecce Homo* and a *Persian Sibyl* after Guercino, now in Glasgow (1823, inv. 312); a

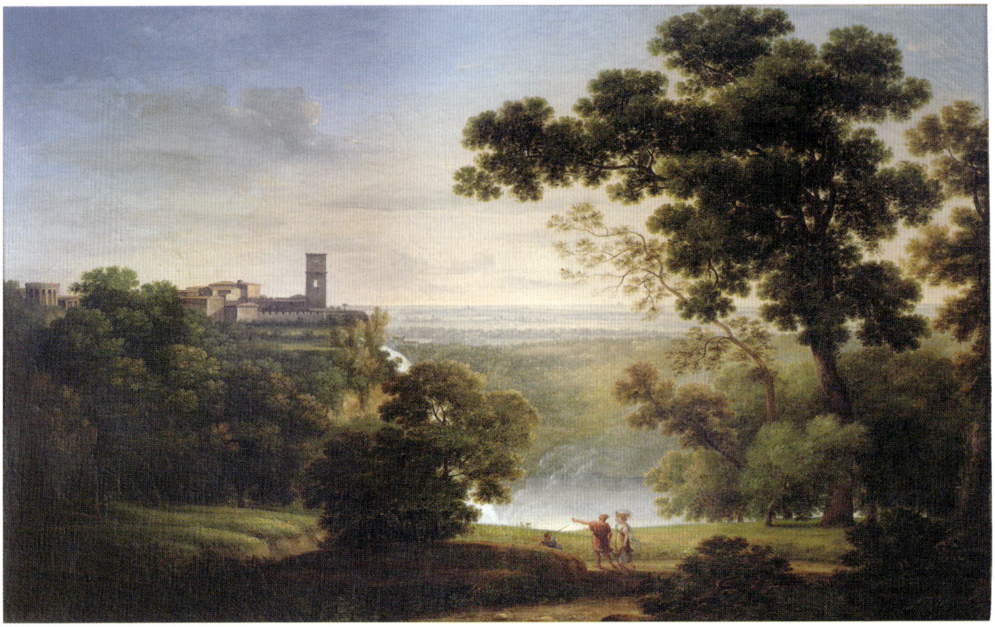

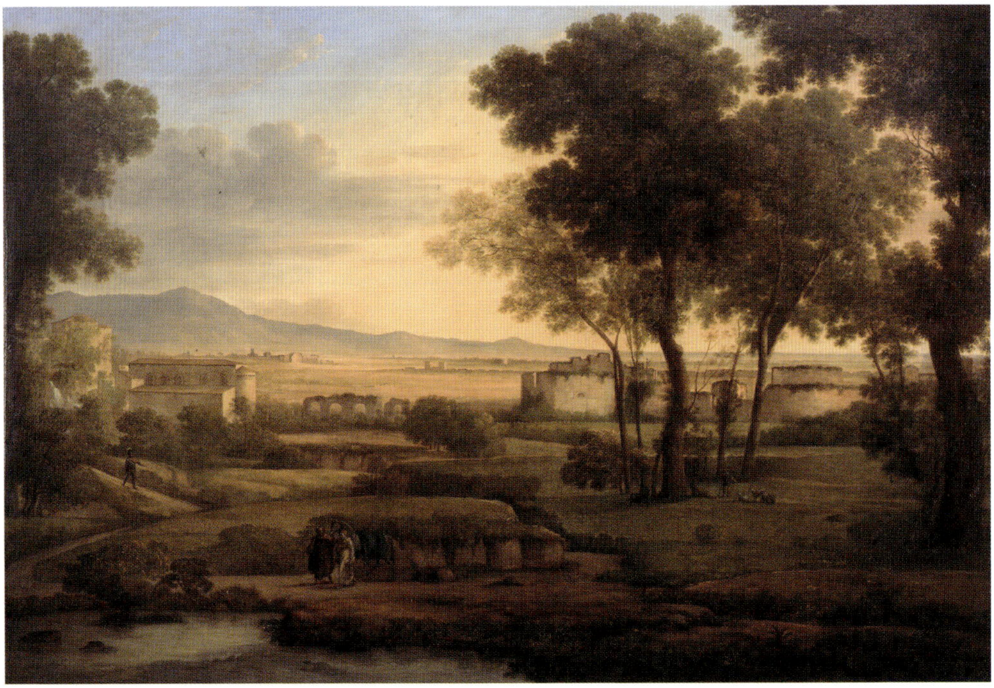

Rosa Mezzera, *The Waterfalls at Tivoli* and *Sunset in the Roman Countryside*, *c.* 1809 and 1811–12. Milan, Accademia di Belle Arti di Brera.

Holy Family after Federico Barocci; a *Cumacan Sibyl* after Domenichino, again in Glasgow (1823, inv. 311). One of her copies after Guido Reni is in the church of St. James in Thornes, West Yorkshire.

Anna Muschi also worked as a draughtswoman, as shown by the title page of the Italian edition of James Thomson's *The Seasons* (1700–1748), translated and published by Patrizio Muschi. Signed and dated Rome 1825, the sheet was engraved by Marco Zignani and Raffaele Morghen.

In the same year she met Abraham Teerlink (Dordrecht, 1776 – Rome, 1857), a Dutch landscape painter, whom she married in 1836. During their twenty years of marriage the couple lived in Via Capo le Case no. 3, in the parish of Sant'Andrea delle Fratte, establishing a circle of international artists and intellectuals frequented by Vincenzo Camuccini, Massimo d'Azeglio, Pietro Tenerani, Giovan Battista Canevari and Bertel Thorvaldsen among others.

In the *Guida generale* by Aldo Marchetti, Anna Muschi is still reported at the same address in 1882. She died in Rome in 1885 and was buried in the Verano Monumental Cemetery.

BIBLIOGRAPHY: Salvatore Di Salvo, "Le sorelle Muschi di Casteldelpiano pittrici ed i loro famigliari: i pittori A. Teerlink e G.B. Canvari, l'archittetto." *Amiata. Storia e territorio* 20, no. 57 (2008), 6–20.

Consuelo Lollobrigida

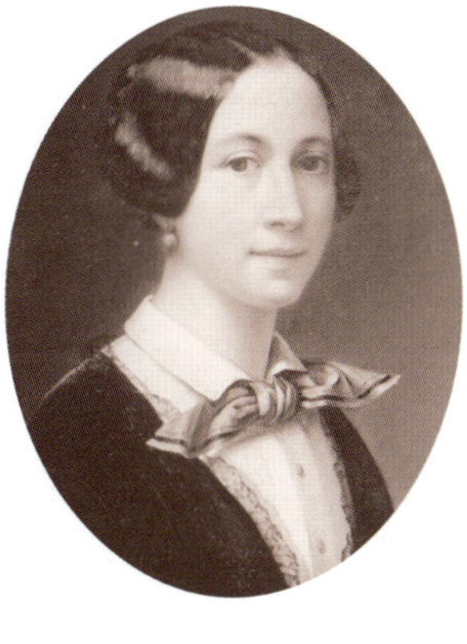

Émile-Françoise Paulien (Rouillon)

(Paris, 1822 – Romaìe, 1912)

Émile (also Emilie or Emilia) Françoise Paulien was born in Paris in 1822. Rouillon, the last name with which she usually signed her works, was that of her husband Pierre-Joseph.

In 1851 she was elected member of the Congregazione dei Virtuosi al Pantheon, presented by the artist Giovanni Silvagni, her teacher. On 13 March 1853 she sent her self-portrait to the same confraternity; its signature, date and the indication of the place (*Emilia Rouillon/Roma 1852*), document her presence in Rome at least from this time as well as certifying its authorship. In the *Almanacco* of 1855 her studio is described as located in Borgo San Pietro no. 162, or 172, as reported a few years later in a guide to Rome for travellers.

Rouillon specialized in executing copies of artists from the early Renaissance to the mid-17th century, an academic practice aimed at demonstrating her own capabilities as a painter in the hope of establishing herself on the collectors' market.

In the catalogue of the *Salon de Paris* of 1869, the list of the drawings section includes a watercolour by her (belonging to M. Lecointe), entitled *Child* and drawn from Raphael's work in the Gallery of the Accademia di San Luca. The biographical notes indicate that she was a student of M. Conterani in Rome and could be contacted in Paris "at the premises of M. Goupil, rue Chaptal 9", a probable reference to the auction house of the same name based at this address.

The catalogue of the *Salon* of 1870 mentions another two watercolours: *The Virgin of Spoleto*, after Giovanni di Pietro called Lo Spagna (belonging to M. W. Fol) and *La Fornarina*, a tribute to the famous painting by Raphael now in the Galleria Nazionale di Palazzo Barberini.

In the same year her name appeared in the catalogue of objects admitted to the *Esposizione romana relativa all'arte cristiana e al culto cattolico*, with a painting depicting *Our Lord Jesus Christ in the House of Simon the Pharisee*. In 1869 she took part in the exhibition organized by the Società amatori e cultori delle belle arti with two portraits.

Rouillon is also known for having portrayed a number of very different sitters: Harriet Hopkins (1867); M. Charles Louis Édouard Bouillat (1883), the French consul to Glasgow, Antwerp and Milan; the sculptor James Henry Helsetine (1868); the general Joseph Édouard de La Motte-Rouge (Château de La Motte-Rouge, Hénansal).

Antonio Borgogna, a lawyer and philanthropist, and founder of the Museo Borgogna (1907), collected some of her watercolours. Additionally, an *Allegory of Dawn* (1868) is reportedly in the Musée d'art et d'histoire (MAH) in Geneva (inv. CR 0414).

Rouillon died in Rome in her apartment in Palazzo Borghese a Ripetta; she was buried at the Verano cemetery on 15 May 1912.

BIBLIOGRAPHY: Anna Lisa Genovese, "Diario 1852–1877." In Vitaliano Tiberia, *La Congregazione dei Virtuosi al Pantheon da Pio VII a Pio IX*. Galatina: Congedo, 2015, 689; Michela Gianfranceschi, "Diario 1837–1851." In Vitaliano Tiberia, *La Congregazione dei Virtuosi al Pantheon da Pio VII a Pio IX*. Galatina: Congedo, 2015, 669 and no. 152.

Alice Militello

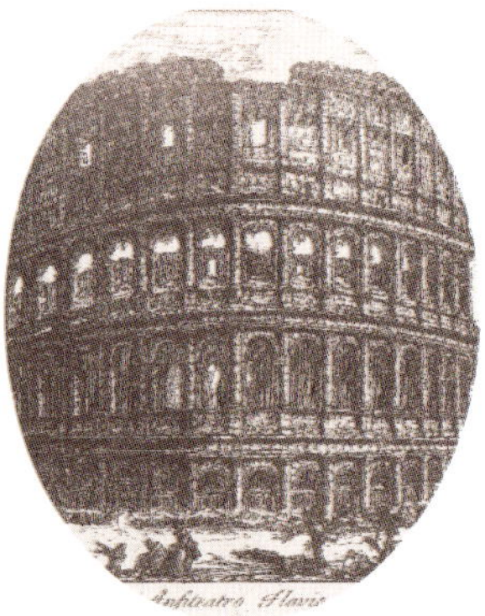

Laura Piranesi
(Rome, 1754–1790)

Laura Piranesi, the eldest child of Giovanni Battista (Venice, 1720 – Rome, 1778) and of Angelica Pasquini (Angela in some documents), was born in Rome in the late summer of 1754. From the certificate of her baptism, celebrated in the church of San Francesco ai Monti on 17 September 1754, we learn the name of her godfather, Monsignor Guido Bottari, brother of the more famous Gaetano, Piranesi's protector after his arrival from Venice. In 1761 she moved with her family to Palazzo Tomati in Strada Felice (Via Sistina no. 48) where Giovanni Battista began to produce his own prints, abandoning his collaboration with the bookseller Giovanni Bouchard. Laura thus grew up breathing the atmosphere of her father's workshop alongside her brother Francesco, four years younger (Rome, 1758 – Paris, 1810). While Francesco was steered by their father towards archaeological studies, Laura trained as an engraver, particularly of *vedute*. This was a very popular genre among the foreign *grandtourists* who frequented the Piranesi studio, especially those from England, interested in archaeological finds. Her production of prints has been neglected by critics with the exception of the major repertoires of engravings, which always mention her with her brother Francesco. Her oeuvre consists of around twenty small views of ancient and modern Roman monuments, all etchings (measuring around mm 130 × 200), signed "Laura (or "Lavora") Piranesi". Most are copies with variations of her father's larger views. These works are often contained in collective albums with those of her father and brother, and were published after Giovanni Battista's death, probably by Francesco who had inherited their father's print workshop. On the death of their father, he paid out a dowry much smaller than Laura's share of the inheritance; she married shortly afterwards (December 1778). Her husband was Josef Schwerzmann, a cabinetmaker of Swiss origin with whom she opened some shops in Via Frattina that later went bankrupt. In 1780 their only daughter Luisa Clara was born; when Francesco died, she claimed a share of Piranesi's legacy on her mother's behalf. Pursued by his debtors, Josef was forced to go into hiding. Laura became ill and died on 9 March 1790, and was buried in Santa Susanna. Laura's drawing style is freer and lighter than that of her father. She does not use a ruling pen, her drawings are executed freehand, and she seems to prefer a single acid bath, with a formal balance of whites and blacks that is less dramatic and more picturesque compared with her father's works.

BIBLIOGRAPHY: Rita Bernini, "Laura Piranesi 'incise': A Woman Printmaker Following in her Father's Footsteps." In *Female Printmakers, Printsellers, and Print Publishers in the Eighteenth-Century. The Imprint of Women c. 1700–1830*, ed. by Cristina S. Martinez, Cynthia E. Roman. Cambridge: Cambridge University Press, 2024, 123–36.

Rita Bernini

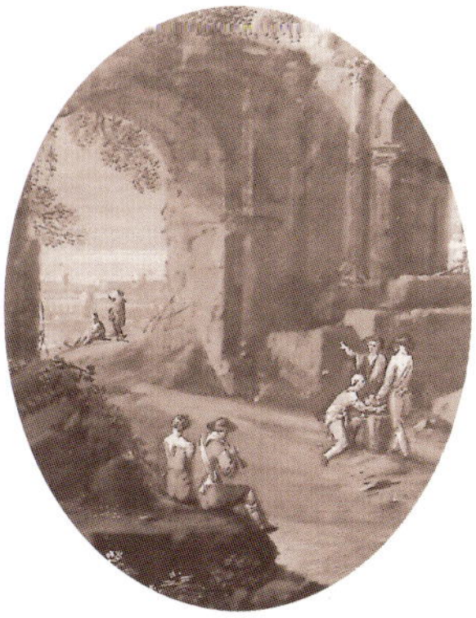

Maria Luigia Raggi

(Genoa, *ante* 1742–1813)

Battina Maria Ignazia was born in Genoa and was baptized on 15 February 1742 in the parish church of San Marcellino. The daughter of Marquis Giovan Antonio and of Maria Brignole Sale, sister of Gian Francesco Maria (1695–1760), Doge of Genoa from 1746 to 1748, Maria Luigia was the first known woman landscape artist in the history of Italian art. She entered the convent school of the Incarnazione in Genoa at the age of nine as Battina Ignazia and was later forced to become a nun. She devoted her whole life to painting, learned thanks to the teachings of Maria Castello, also the private governess of her sister Isabellina.

The discovery of four *Landscapes with Ruins*, initialled "MLR" and signed "MARIA LUISA RAGGI" or "L. RAGGI", has made it possible to identify the anonymous Master of the Prato Capricci, also known as the Eighteenth-Century Landscape Painter of Roman Ruins or Pseudo-Anesi, and to ascribe to her four works in the Musei Capitolini and the substantial corpus in the Musei Civici of Prato.

Between 1781 and 1783, the painter is documented in Rome in Palazzo Raggi al Corso, owned by her uncle Ferdinando, an intellectual, artist and architect elected member of the Accademia di San Luca in 1775 and its president in 1781.

During her stay in Rome, Maria Luigia painted capricci and landscapes, including the rare *View of the Colosseum* on a fan-shaped support, in the collection of the Parco Archeologico del Colosseo since 2021. Of the same period are the two *Capricci* in the Accademia di San Luca, probable *pièces de reception* executed during Ferdinando's presidency. Also belonging to her Roman period are the four *Capricci* in the Musei Capitolini, formerly in the collection of the Castellani, a well known family of goldsmiths and collectors who had their shop next to that of Maria Luigia, in the since-demolished Vicolo Cacciabove in the Palazzo Raggi complex.

In 1783 the artist nun is again documented in Genoa, where Ferdinando Raggi sent her money, perhaps the proceeds from the sale of her works left in Rome and aimed at the flourishing market of Grand Tour collectors.

She died in Genoa on 25 March 1823 and was buried in the cemetery of the convent of the Incarnazione. Her tomb was destroyed during the bombings of the city during the Second World War.

BIBLIOGRAPHY: Sergio Guarino, "Maria Luigia Raggi (Maestro dei Capricci di Prato)." In *Pinacoteca Capitolina. Catalogo generale*, ed. by Sergio Guarino, Patrizia Masini. Milan: Electa, 2006, 488–91; Consuelo Lollobrigida, *Maria Luigia Raggi. Il Capriccio Paesaggistico tra Arcadia e Grand Tour.* Rome: Budai, 2012.

Consuelo Lollobrigida

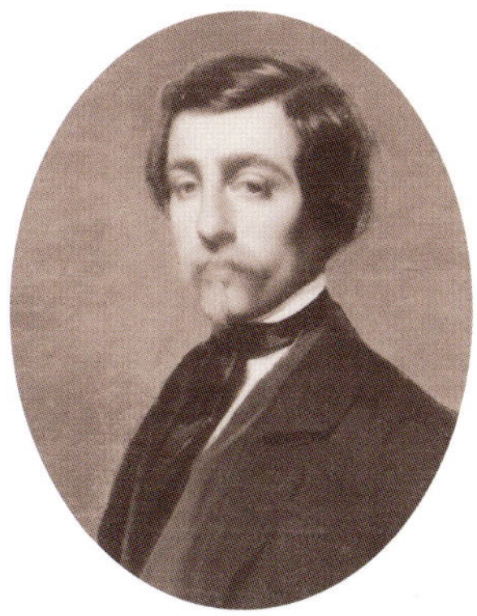

Joséphine-Cécile Raoul-Rochette (Calamatta)

(Paris, 1817–1893)

The granddaughter of the Neoclassical sculptor Jean-Antoine Houdon and daughter of the director of the Cabinet of Medals Raoul-Rochette, Joséphine is known as a painter. Her work as an artist focused on genre painting and portraiture. She trained first under the Neoclassical wing of Hippolyte Flandrin, through whom she was influenced by Jean-Auguste-Dominique Ingres, and then with Luigi Calamatta, a famous engraver (and her husband from 1840). She was also interested in the Italian Renaissance and the

Spanish 17th century, studying Bartolomé Esteban Murillo in particular. Her presence in Rome is not attested before 1840, when she arrived in Italy with her husband Luigi on their honeymoon. Two years later their only daughter Lina was born; she later married the son of George Sand, Maurice. Her godfather was Ingres. In 1841 the two Calamatta went to Villa Medici to meet its new director Victor Schnetz, whom they encountered again in 1844. In the same year, with her husband, Joséphine was elected member of the Virtuosi al Pantheon. She probably accompanied her husband and his students on their study visits to the Raphael Rooms in the Vatican. She is no longer attested in Rome after the breakup of her marriage and divorce from Luigi (1852–1853). She took holy orders in 1888 and died in Paris in 1893. Her *Portrait of Luigi Calamatta* of 1842 is on display in Rome at the Accademia di San Luca (inv. 822). She herself gave the painting to the Accademia in 1872, shortly after the death of her husband three years earlier. By contrast, her *Portrait of Desiré Raoul-Rochette* in the Alessandro Cialdi collection (inv. 8668) is known thanks to an 1853 engraving by Luigi. The work was painted by his daughter in 1843, as reported by the inscription beneath the print "Painted by J. Calamatta née R-R 1843".

BIBLIOGRAPHY: Enrica Foschi, *Luigi Calamatta e la collezione Alessandro Cialdi di Civitavecchia.* Tarquinia: Lamberti, 2018, 19, 59, 146.

Laura Palombaro

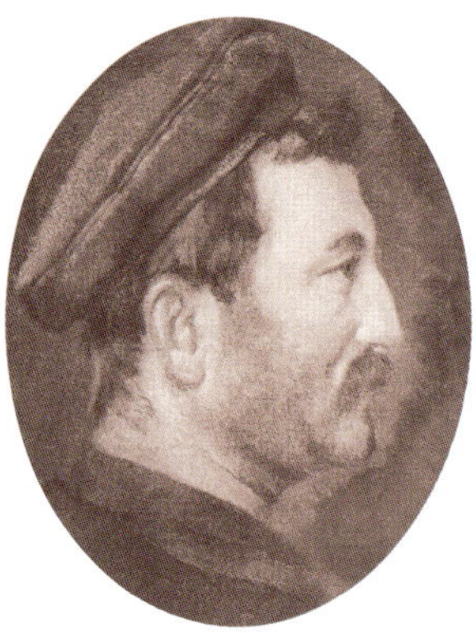

EMMA REGIS

(Turin, 1854 – Rome, after 1934)

Even today, little is known about the life of Emma Regis. Periodical publications of the early 20th century such as magazines or commercial guides add to the information available on the artist and move the date of her death forward to at least the early 1930s. A painter of Torinese origin, but active in Rome, she was the daughter of General Gioachino Regis (1811–1886). The *Guida numismatica universale* of 1889, which mentions her as heir to her father's collection of ancient coins, confirms that she lived in Rome in Piazza Monte d'Oro no. 29. At least between 1894 and 1932, Emma had a studio at Via Margutta no. 53b (*Annuario d'Italia* 1894, *Annuario Italiano* 1932 and commercial guides in the chronological interval). Oddly, in 1899 alone her address is reported as Piazza San Marco no. 16 (*Annuario d'Italia* 1899). Recorded in the printed sources essentially as a portraitist, very few of her works are known, almost all in private collections. Her best-known painting remains the *Madonna of the Thistle* of 1929, owned by the Istituto Romano San Michele and recently restored (2020–21).

BIBLIOGRAPHY: Laura Caterina Cherubini, "Da via Sallustina a via del Lavatore: per luoghi con gli artisti." In *Tutte le strade portano a Roma?*, exhib. cat. (Rome 1993), ed. by Valentina Bonomo. Rome: Carte Segrete, 1993, 38.

Tiziano Casola

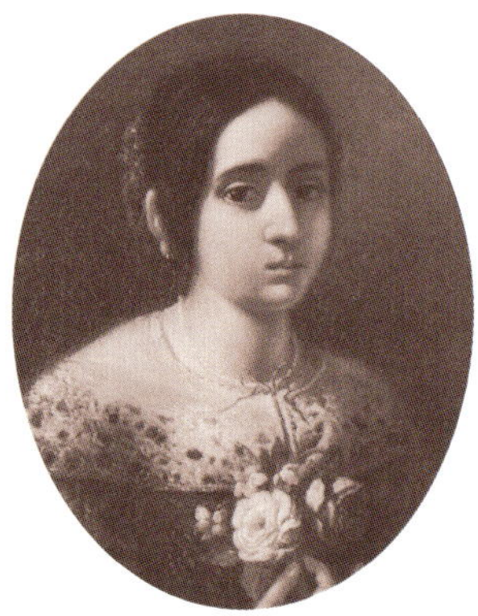

MARTA ROSA

(Rome, second half of the 17th century)

The only information on the career of Marta Rosa is provided by Lione Pascoli, whose biography of her father Francesco Rosa (1638–1687) recounts how "as a little girl she was fond of painting and began to draw at the age of ten and to paint at twelve. There are many paintings executed by her". The only work identified by the biographer is a

Joséphine-Cécile Raoul-Rochette (Calamatta), *Portrait of Lucio Lelli*, c. 1848–52. Alessandra Masu Collection.

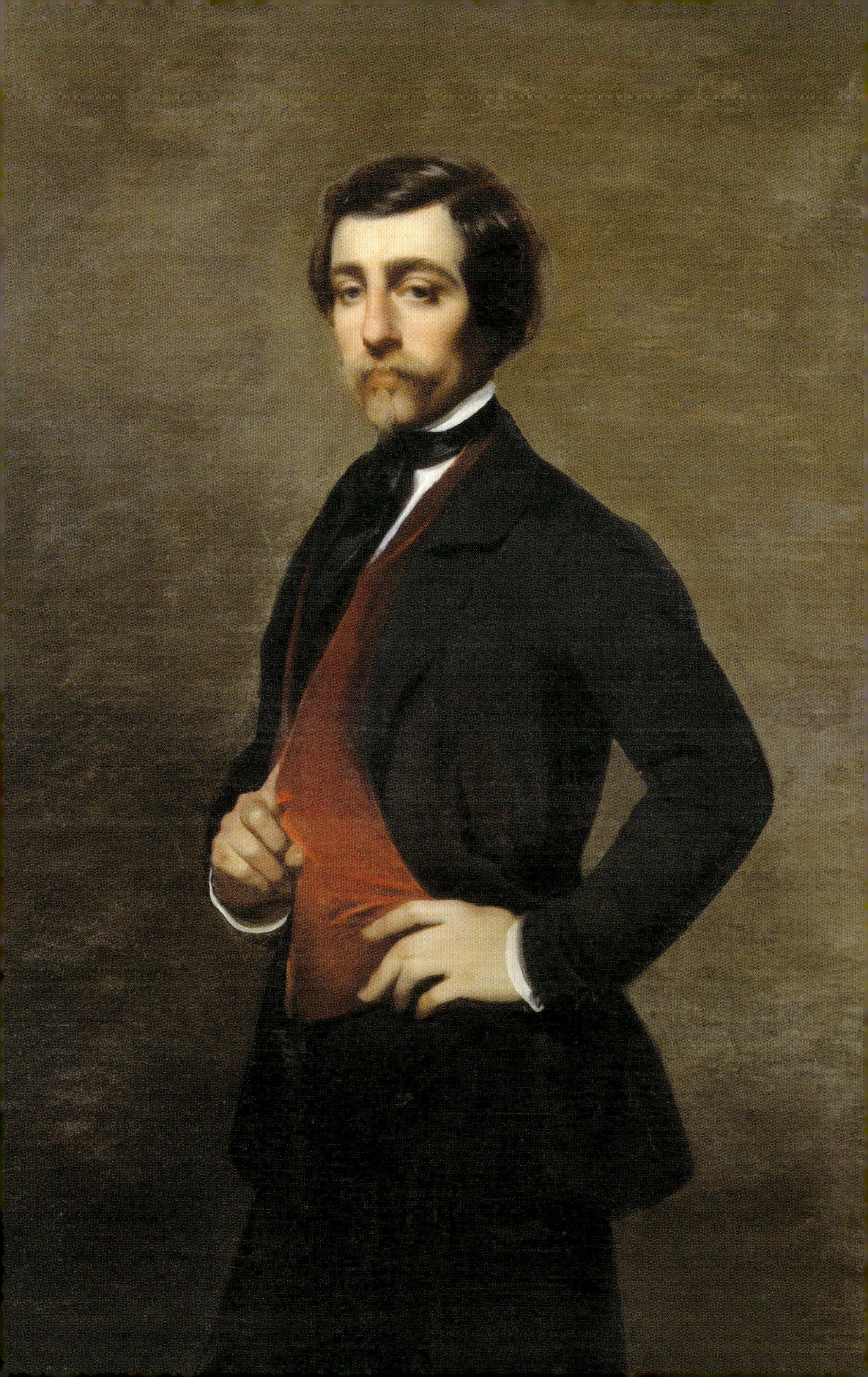

Crucifixion, which "she painted at the age of seventeen, measuring ten *palmi* and seven, copied from one executed by her father (Rome, Accademia Nazionale di San Luca, inv. 428). This copy was placed on an altar outside Rome". Unfortunately, given the lack of more specific information it has not yet been possible to trace this work. As the source tells us, Marta was highly educated and "resembled her father both in face and in talent". Again according to the biographer, she married Giovanni Olivetani and died in childbirth when she was thirty-two.

The presence of a portrait of her executed by her father in the collections of the Accademia di San Luca makes it likely that she frequented this institution. She is also recorded as a member in the papers of the Compagnia di San Giuseppe in Terrasanta (later known as the Congregazione dei Virtuosi del Pantheon), of which her father and her brother Sigismondo were official members.

BIBLIOGRAPHY: Giulia De Marchi, "Fabio Rosa benefattore dell'Accademia di San Luca: in ricordo di Olivier Michel accademico benemerito." *Annali delle arti e degli archivi* 3 (2017), 288–89.

Ilaria Arcangeli

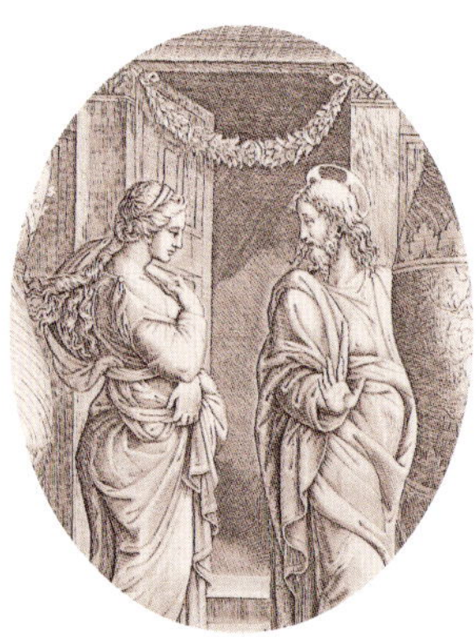

Diana Scultori, called Diana Mantovana

(Mantua, *c.* 1547 – Rome, 1612)

Diana Scultori, called Diana Mantovana, was born in Mantua in around 1547. She was trained as an engraver together with her brother Adamo by their father, Giovanni Battista de Spinchieris called Scultori (1503–1575), and became one of the main interpreters of Giulio Romano's oeuvre in the city. Diana's remarkable talents as an engraver were praised for the first time by Giorgio Vasari in the second edition of his *Lives of the Artists* following their meeting in Mantua in 1566.

The artist's presence in Rome is attested at least since 1575. In this year she obtained a papal privilege from Gregory XIII Boncompagni giving her the exclusive right to sign and market five of her prints for ten years; she was the first woman printmaker to obtain such a concession. In the same year she dedicated her *Christ and the Woman Taken in Adultery* to Eleonora of Austria, Duchess of Mantua. An initial three engravings, based on works by Giulio Romano and probably already executed in Mantua, are accompanied by a further two: a *St Jerome* after a lost original drawing by Daniele di Volterra and a *Nativity*, or *Sacrifice of Isaac*, after Giulio Clovio.

In Rome, Diana embarked on a profitable commercial career dedicated to publicizing the designs of her husband, the architect Francesco da Volterra (1535–1594) in engravings; the two were already married in 1575 and both achieved considerable success. Diana's time in Rome gave her the opportunity to study the models of ancient statuary; her engraving of the *Hercules with the Golden Apples*, after the gilded bronze sculpture in the Musei Capitolini, was included in an edition of the *Speculum romanae magnificentiae* (1581).

Three years after giving birth to her only known child, Giovanni Battista, Diana was admitted to the Congregazione dei Virtuosi al Pantheon in 1580. After the death of her husband, she was married again to the architect Giulio Pelosi in 1596.

Her last two dated works were executed in 1588: the *Visitation* after Vasari and the *Deposition* after Paris Nogari (both lost). After this, no other works by the artist are known. She died in Rome in 1612.

At the current state of research, Diana is credited with sixty-three certain engravings and a number of uncertain works, and her production includes prints based on ancient, religious, mythological, architectural and allegorical subjects.

BIBLIOGRAPHY: Anna Lisa Genovese, "DIARIO 1800–1834." In Vitaliano Tiberia, *La Congregazione dei Virtuosi al Pantheon da Pio VII a Pio IX*. Galatina: Congedo, 2015, 273–74.

Maria Giulia Rinaldi

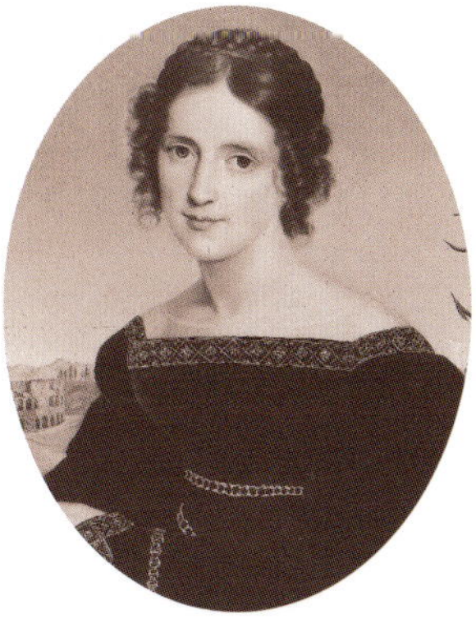

Luise Seidler

(Jena, 1786 – Weimar, 1866)

The daughter of an academic from Jena, from a very early age Luise entered the city's intellectual circles which at the time included illustrious figures such as Friedrich Schiller, Johann Gottlieb Fichte, Georg Wilhelm Friedrich Hegel, Friedrich Wilhelm Joseph Schelling, and the brothers Alexander and Wilhelm von Humboldt. During the Napoleonic occupation of Jena from 1806–1807, Luise married a member of the French troops but moved to Dresden shortly after being widowed in 1810. Here she developed a desire to become a painter and trained first under Christian Leberecht Vogel and then with Gerhard von Kügelgen. From Weimar to Dresden, her talent aroused enthusiasm and earned widespread respect, among others from Johann Wolfgang von Goethe, whom she met through the publisher Carl Friedrich Ernst Frommann. Active essentially as a copyist and portraitist – in 1811 for the family of Duke August of Saxe-Gotha-Altenburg – she was helped by Goethe to obtain a scholarship to continue her studies in Munich in 1817 and then a travel bursary to Italy. She lived here between 1818 and 1823 (when she returned to Weimar because her father was seriously ill). In Rome, she frequented Northern European circles and was hosted in the houses of the Prussian ambassador Barthold Georg Niebuhr and of von Humboldt's wife. This brought her into contact with the Nazarene painters, in whose 1819 exhibition at Villa Caffarelli she participated, displaying the *Portrait of Fanny Caspers* (Copenaghen, Thorvaldsens Museum, B 440). Between 1819 and 1821, she spent several months in Naples and Florence, where she copied Raphael's *Madonna del Granduca* and *Madonna of the Goldfinch* for Grand Duke Karl August. Several of her known copies of old master paintings date to her time in Rome. On her return to Weimar, recommended by Goethe and Johann Heinrich Meyer, Duke Karl August entrusted her with the education of his daughters and appointed her custodian of the Grand Ducal collection. Always appreciated in society circles, she maintained her friendship with Philipp Veit and Friedrich Preller, an admirer of her copies. In old age her increasing blindness made it impossible for her to work. Before she died, she wrote her autobiography: *Erinnerungen und Leben der Malerin Louise Seidler*, published in Berlin in 1874.

BIBLIOGRAPHY: Bärbel Kovalevski, *Louise Seidler 1786-1866: Goethes geschätzte Malerin.* Berlin: Kovalevski, 2007; Sylke Kaufmann, *Louise Seidler (1786-1866) – Leben und Werk: mit einem Œuvreverzeichnis ihrer Ölgemälde, Pastelle und bildmäßigen Zeichnungen.* 2 vols. Bucha bei Jena: Quartus-Verlag, 2016, 1:130–219.

Tiziano Casola

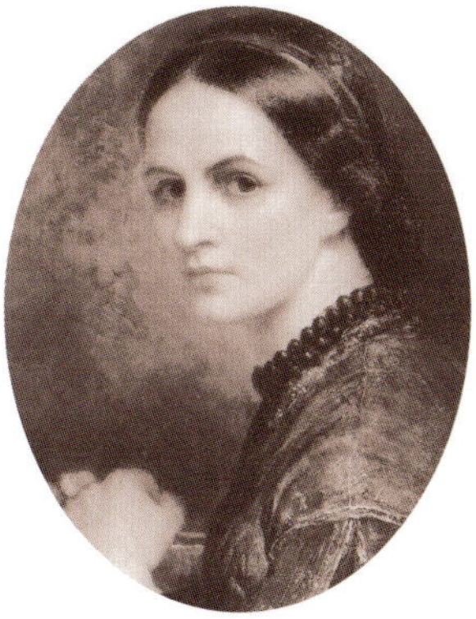

Ann Mary Severn (Newton)

(Rome, 1832 – London, 1866)

The daughter of the painter Joseph Severn (1793–1879), Ann Mary spent her early childhood in Via Rasella no. 152. Her father, who had arrived in Rome in 1820 with the poet John Keats, was at the time one of the most active members of the Anglo-Roman community. From him Ann Mary received her early education, like her brothers Walter and Arthur, also painters. In 1841, at the age of nine, Ann Mary moved with her family to London. Here she later became the student of George Richmond and specialized in portraits of children,

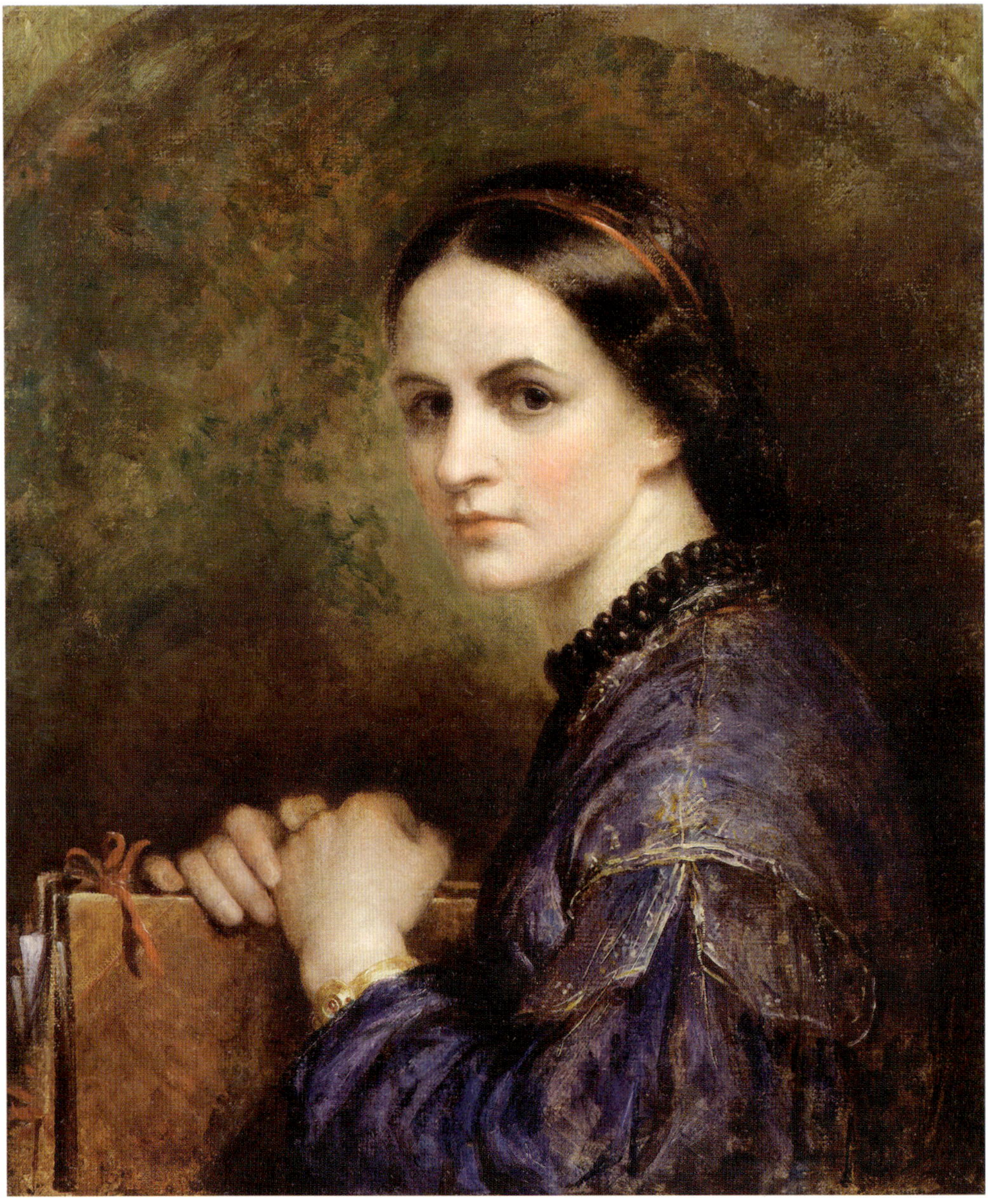

Ann Mary Severn (Newton), *Self-Portrait*, *c.* 1862. Galles, Denbighshire, Bodelwyddan Castle (long-term loan from London, National Portrait Gallery).

Anna Stanchi, *Garland of Flowers with Venus and Adonis*, 1647. Private Collection.

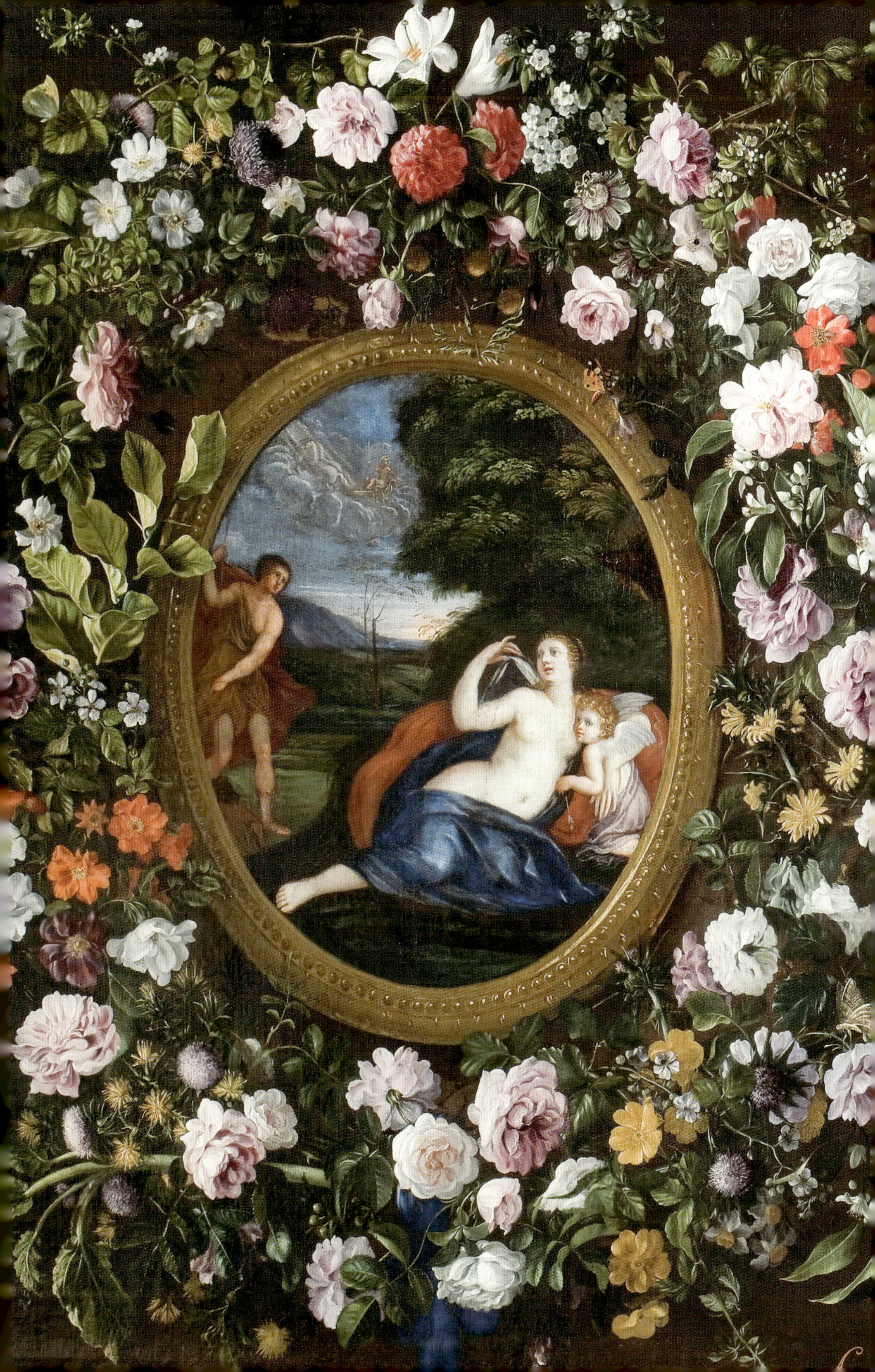

working in pastel, chalk and watercolour. In the mid-1850s, thanks to a series of important commissions, she managed to support her family, which was in financial difficulty. Among many others, she portrayed the children of Queen Victoria (the portraits of princesses Beatrice, Helena Augusta Victoria and Louise Caroline Alberta are known through the prints made from them by Richard James Lane: London, National Portrait Gallery, inv. NPG D22112 and D22135). During a stay in Paris in 1857 she received lessons from Ary Scheffer. In 1861, coinciding with her father's return to Rome as British consul, Ann Mary married the archaeologist Charles Thomas Newton (1816–1894), later Keeper of Greek and Roman antiquities at the British Museum and consul in Greece. For him she executed illustrations for lectures and publications (*History of the Discoveries at Helicarnassus, Cnidus, and Branchidae*, 1862–1863; *Travels and Discoveries in the Levant*, 1865). With her husband, she visited the eastern Mediterranean, documenting their travels in sketches. Between 1852 and 1865, Ann Mary is attested among the participants in the annual exhibitions of the Royal Academy of Art. She died prematurely of measles, without having had children. Queen Victoria remembered her in her *Journal* (7 January 1866) as "a pretty, clever young artist, who painted several of the family & did also beautiful copies of the Old Masters".

BIBLIOGRAPHY: Lionel Henry Cust, s.v. "Newton, Ann Mary." In *Oxford Dictionary of National Biography*, ed. by Colin Matthew, Brian Harrison. Vol. 50. Oxford: Oxford University Press, 2004; Grant F. Scott, *Joseph Severn. Letters and Memoirs*. London-New York: Routledge, 2016, 107, 118–19, 408, 488, 497, 507, 509, 512–13; Debbie Challis, "The Ghosts of Ann Mary Severn Newton: Grief, an Imagines Life and (Auto)biography." In Gabriel Moshenska, Clare Lewis, *Life-Writing in the History of Archaeology: Critical Perspectives*. London: UCL Press, 2023, 379–403, no. 3.15.

Tiziano Casola

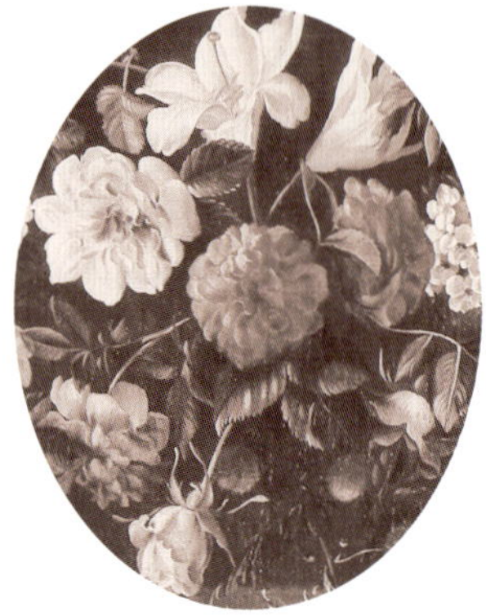

Anna Stanchi

(Rome, 1613?–1681)

The painter Anna Stanchi was rediscovered only after the appearance on the art market of two paintings that she signed and dated (Amsterdam, Sotheby's, 8 May 2007, lot 96; Paris, Christie's, 23 June 2010, lot 19). She was immediately identified as a member of the Stanchi family, composed of the three brothers Giovanni, Niccolò and Angelo, whose activity as still life painters is documented by archival sources and by numerous paintings ascribed to them by the studies. New documents make it possible to establish that Anna was the second oldest, born probably in around 1613. From 1641 onwards, the four siblings lived in Via Paolina together with Anna's husband, Claudio Pionier, a French artist, also recorded in the same street in the preceding years. The couple had two children (Giovanni Ludovico and Anna Maria); after her husband's death in 1647, Anna was remarried to the Genoese Cristoforo Galletti and moved with him to Vicolo Leona. She was never described as a *pittora*, or painter, in the parish registers, but in the 1644 census the profession of "painters" is ascribed to the entire family.

The information of greatest help in circumscribing the artist's career are the inscriptions (on the bottom right in both paintings) which also give the place, Rome, and the dates of 1643 and 1647. The signature clearly indicates Anna's intention to assert her role within the workshop where, as shown by the studies on the other members of the family, the siblings worked in close collaboration. The minimal age gap between Anna and Giovanni, always considered the head of the workshop, alongside the very high quality of both of her signed works and the fact that the two lived together for a long time, raise further questions about the workshop's management. Indeed, numerous flower paintings ascribed to Giovanni, or more generically to a male Stanchi and in just one case to a female Stanchi (Chigi Inventory), are recorded in the inventories of important Roman collections. We do not have sufficient information to establish if Anna specialized exclusively in flower painting or if she also worked on other types of figurative subjects. It is highly likely that she also contributed to various paintings hitherto attributed to her brothers.

BIBLIOGRAPHY: Alberto Crispo, "Pietro Paolo Cennini e la bottega degli Stanchi." *Parma per l'arte*, new ser. 19 (2013), 63–70.

Ilaria Arcangeli

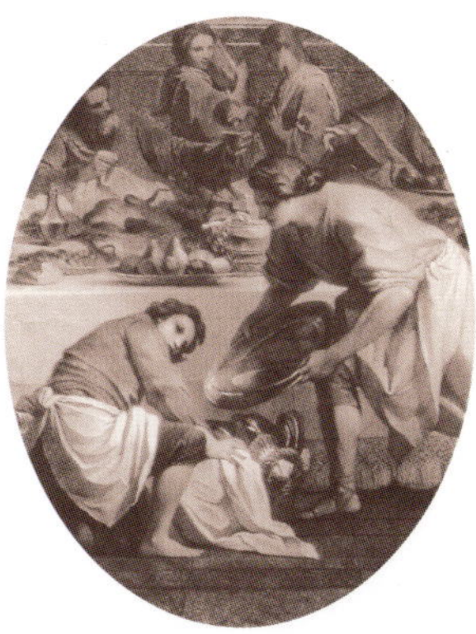

Maria Felice Tibaldi (Subleyras)

(Rome, 1707–1770)

The daughter of the famous violinist Giovanni Battista Tibaldi (*c.* 1670–1755), Maria Felice studied from a very early age with Abbot Giuseppe Felice Ramelli, "in his time the most talented miniaturist in the entire world". Already at the age of ten, according to sources of the period, Tibaldi was supporting her family with her work, making up for her father's waning popularity on the Roman music scene. When her teacher died, the artist sold his works for over 80 Roman *scudi*. In 1742 she became a member of the Accademia di San Luca in Rome and, the following year, with the name of Asteria Aretusa, of the Arcadian Academy. She specialized in historical subjects, portrait miniatures and copies of old master paintings and modern works, especially those of the French painter Pierre Subleyras (1699–1749) whom she married in 1739. After being widowed at the age of forty, she lived with her family, which she supported thanks to her profession. Trading on a fame that remained intact if not increased, she ran a very popular studio where she worked alongside her sister Teresa and daughter Clementina. Her miniature of the *Dinner at the House of the Pharisee* based on the masterpiece executed by her husband for the refectory of the monastery of Santa Maria Nuova in Asti (Musée du Louvre, inv. 8000), was displayed in the porch of the Pantheon on 19 March 1750. It was purchased two years later by Benedict XIV Lambertini for the sum of 1000 Roman *scudi* and became the first work by a living artist to enter the Capitoline collections (inv. PC 76). During this time, she continued to execute works for the elite of cosmopolitan Rome. Her clients and protectors included figures of the calibre of the Elector Palatine Charles Theodore of Bavaria, and Cardinals Silvio Valenti Gonzaga and Cosimo Imperiali. Recent studies have identified a substantial corpus of miniatures while the pastel works are of uncertain attribution. No painting or document currently confirms her work as a painter, mentioned in several sources.

BIBLIOGRAPHY: O. Michel, in *Pierre Subleyras*, exhib. cat. (Rome–Paris 1987), ed. by Pierre Rosenberg, Olivier Michel. Paris: Réunion des Musée nationaux, 1987, 77–81, 109–12; Nicolas Lesur, *Pierre Subleyras (1699-1749)*. Paris: Arthena, 2023, 83–96, 136–38, 165–76, 443, 456–63, 466, 470–76.

Jessica Calipari

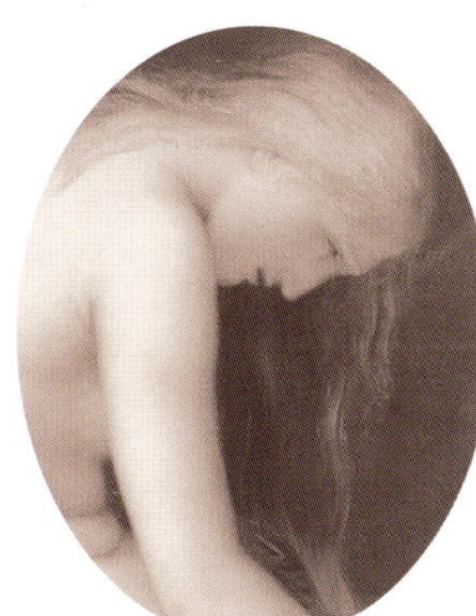

Maria Luigia Vaccolini (Giuli)

(Ravenna, 1749 – Rome, 1811)

Maria Luigia Vaccolini was born in Ravenna in 1749 and settled in Rome after her marriage to Girolamo Giuli in 1780. The couple lived initially in

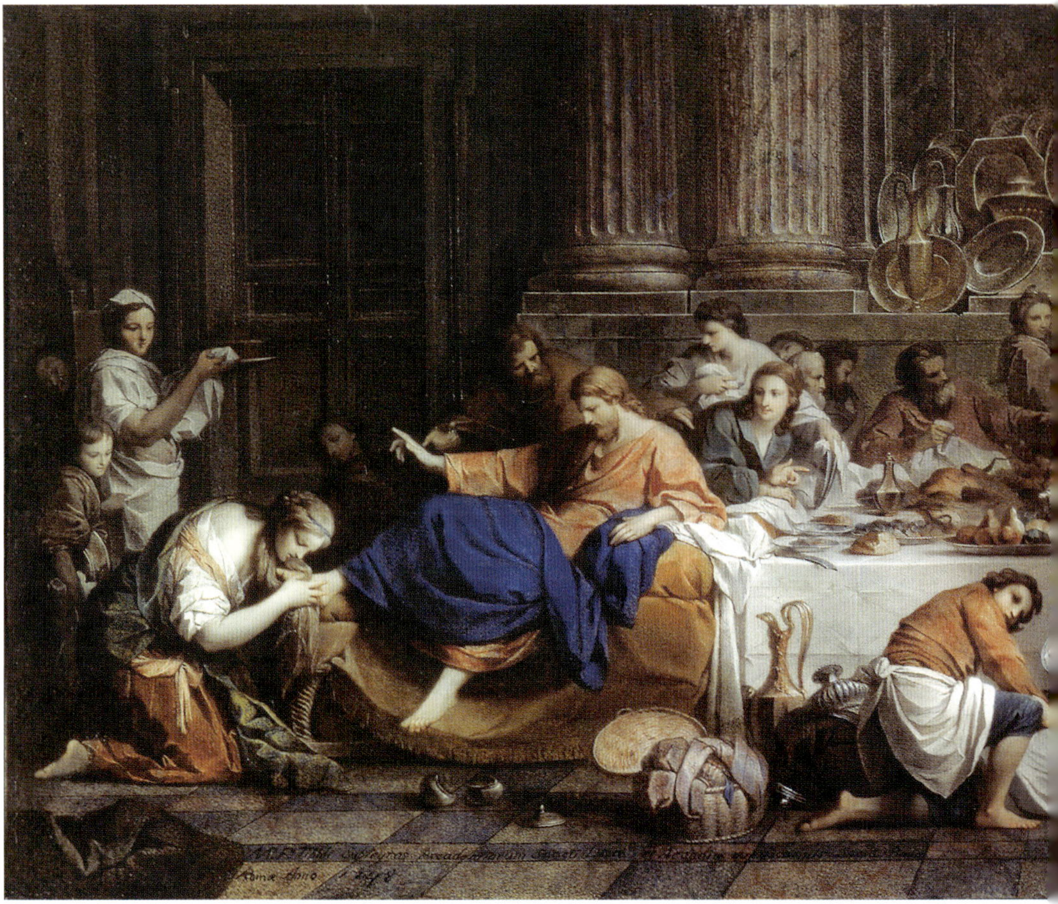

Maria Felice Tibaldi (from Pierre Subleyras), *Dinner at the House of the Pharisee*, 1748.
Rome, Musei Capitolini, Pinacoteca Capitolina.

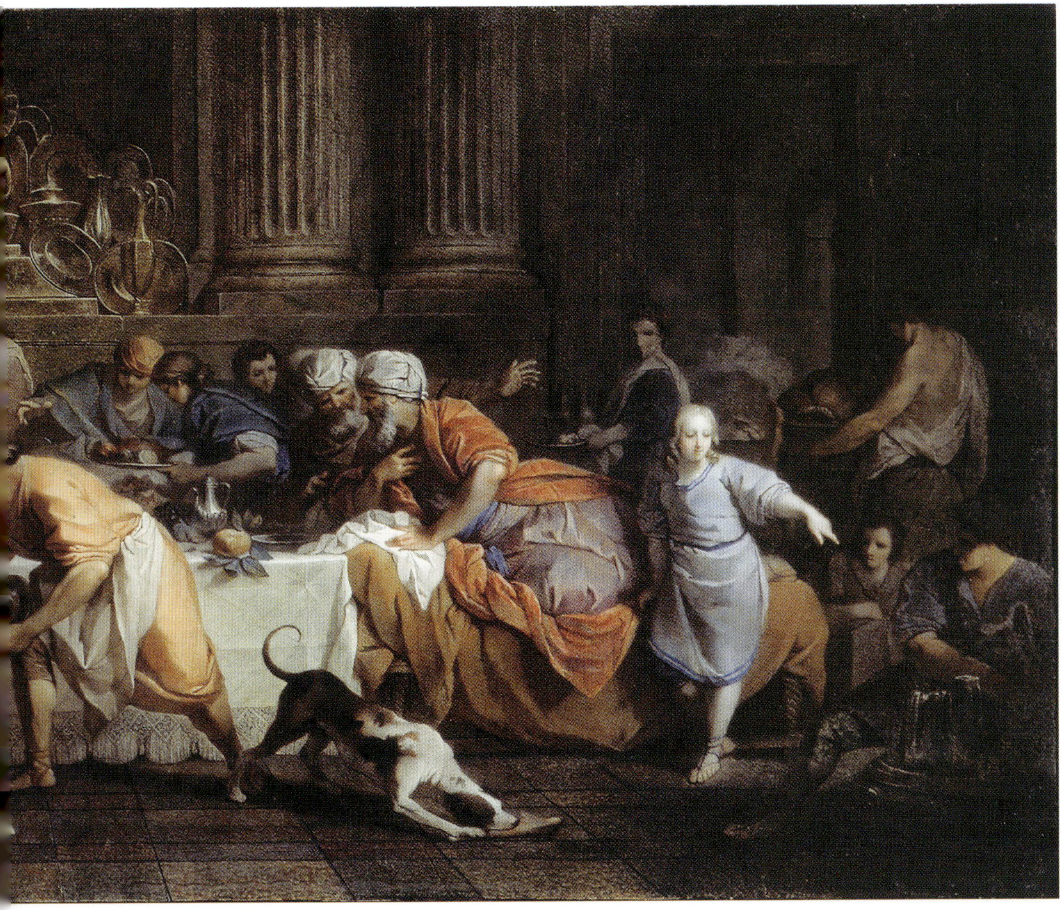

Salita San Giuseppe and then from 1784 onwards is recorded in the parish registers of San Lorenzo in Lucina at the residence of Antonio Canova, for whom the Vaccolini-Giuli kept house. The rapport between Maria Luigia and the master from Possagno intensified between 1785 and 1787, when she helped him to recover after a long illness. However, Maria Luigia's role was not limited to her domestic duties. The sources, including the correspondence and the testimonies of Melchiorre Missirini and Antonio D'Este, recall her privileged position and the sculptor's great respect for her. During the absences of Canova's secretary-biographer, financial transactions and payments were delegated to Maria Luigia. She was also responsible for managing the artist's correspondence, including the letters sent to close friends and those concerning delicate issues of patronage (an example is the copy of the *Psyche* executed for Girolamo Zulian and later purchased by Giuseppe Mangilli). The expression with which Maria Luigia describes it in the letter sent to the Count on 12 July 1794 is as famous as it is elegant: "the plaster is fine, but the marble is enchanting". As well as possessing a "keen intelligence", in the opinion of Antonio D'Este, in administrative tasks, Maria Luigia was also appreciated for her artistic talents. She embarked on a study of drawing and painting, already practiced with some success in the 1790s. In the correspondence of Count Daniele Ippolito degli Oddi, Maria Luigia is often referred to as "our painter", responsible for numerous high-quality copies of Canova's paintings. They include the *Self-Portrait* given to Zulian, who appreciated its "exacting draughtsmanship and tasteful colouring", and that executed for Tiberio Roberti, praised for the "frank concision of its brushstrokes, and the harmony of its draughtsmanship, and the likeness of its subject", as well as the copy of the *Penitent Magdalene* (Rome, Accademia Nazionale di San Luca, inv. 56). In a letter to Pietro Giordani of 20 February 1811, written shortly after Maria Luigia's death, Canova himself ascribed to her "uncommon sense [...], the heart for important masculine matters, [...] a very fine eye for painting and sculpture". A trace of the sculptor's fondness for his housekeeper remains in the design for the Funerary Stele in plaster with the profiles of Maria Luigia and of Canova's mother (1812). Even after her death, the painter helped to enhance the sculptor's fame, as Maria Luigia was the protagonist, with Canova, of a play by Ludovico Muratori staged in Rome in 1877.

BIBLIOGRAPHY: Antonello Cesareo, *Antonio Canova e l'Accademia di San Luca*. Perugia: Morlacchi, 2012, 89–97; Federico Piscopo, *Echi canoviani*. Crespano del Grappa: Parrocchia dei Santi Marco e Pancrazio, 2016, 91–102.

Vanda Lisanti

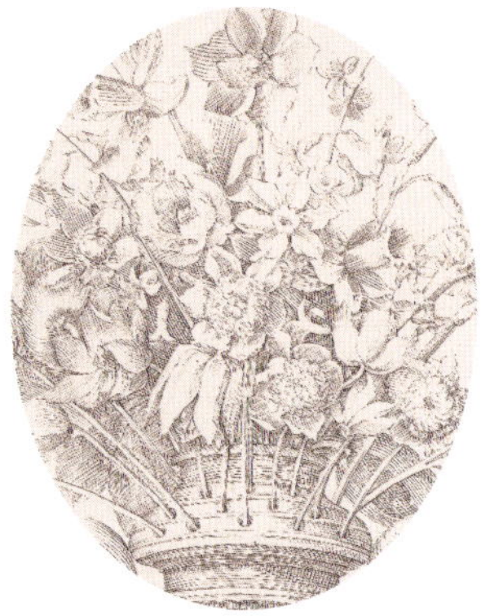

Anna Maria Vaiani

(Milan, *c.* 1604 – Rome, 1654)

Anna Maria Vaiani was born in Milan in around 1604 to the Florentine painter Alessandro Vaiani and Angela Scelpia. At the age of twenty she moved to Rome with her family, starting her artistic career under the guidance of her father as a painter and engraver together with her brother Sebastiano. Her first known work, an etching depicting a *Magdalene*, dates to 1627. In Rome she came into contact with the intellectuals and artists of the time and in 1630, thanks to her friendship with Galileo Galilei and Michelangelo Buonarroti the Younger, she was introduced to the Barberini court. The Barberini family purchased from her a copy of a painting by Titian, a *Madonna with Child and the Young Baptist*, and a work depicting a piece of coral, both now lost. By contrast, still surviving are her engravings for the illustrated botanical treatise *De florum cultura* (1633) by Giovan Battista Ferrari, for which she executed a bouquet of flowers that bears her signature.

In the Barberini entourage, Anna Maria met Cassiano dal Pozzo and collaborated with him on some drawings of antiquities for his *Paper Museum*. In June 1632 she executed three engravings for the *Galleria Giustiniana*: the *Pallas Athena* and the pairs of portrait busts representing Homer and Pindar, and Sappho and Cleopatra. With her father, she worked on the fresco decoration of the chapel of Urban VIII in the Vatican and painted the altarpiece with a *Lamentation Over the Dead Christ*, completing the work on her own after her father's death in 1631.

Anna Maria is recorded in the papers of the Accademia di San Luca in 1630 and 1655, when she participated in a meeting of academic painters with Giustiniana Guidotti, Caterina Ginnasi and Giovanna Garzoni. In 1647 she married the young painter Jacques Courtois, but it was not a happy union. After her husband accused her of abandoning the marriage bed, Anna Maria was arrested and later released thanks to her influential friends at the Barberini court. The couple officially separated in 1653 and Anna Maria's dowry was returned to her.

The artist died in Strada Felice shortly after making her will, on 21 January 1654 at the age of around fifty.

BIBLIOGRAPHY: Lucia Tongiorgi Tomasi, "La «femminil pazienza»: Women Painters and natural History in the Seventeenth and Early Eighteenth Centuries." *Studies in the History of Art* 69 (2008), 164–66; Consuelo Lollobrigida, "Women Artists in Casa Barberini: Plautilla Bricci, Maddalena Corvini, Artemisia Gentileschi, Anna Maria Vaiani, and Virginia da Vezzo." In *Artemisia Gentileschi in a Changing Light*, ed. by Sheila Barker. London–Turnhout: Harvey Miller, 2017, 124–25.

Maria Giulia Rinaldi

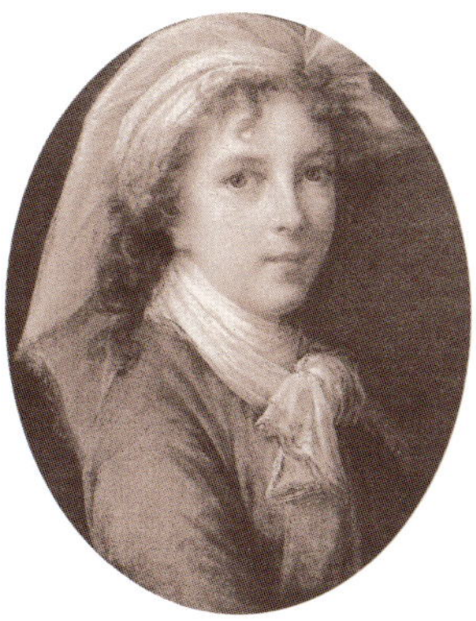

Élisabeth Vigée (Le Brun)

(Paris, 1755–1842)

The daughter of the painter Louis Vigée, a modest pastellist and portraitist, Élisabeth Vigée Le Brun was a precocious and talented artist. A refined interpreter of the tastes of Paris at the time of Louis XVI, appreciated for the natural and lively style of her society portraits, she married the well-known antique dealer Jean-Baptiste-Pierre Le Brun (1748–1813) at the age of twenty. She left France for Italy soon after the storming of the Bastille due to her ties to the royal family and the court of Versailles. She arrived in Rome in November 1789 after a series of brief sojourns in the cities of art through which she passed. Here she found a first temporary home at the Académie de France, then directed by her friend François-Guillaume Ménageot.

As she herself says in her *Souvenirs* (1835–1837) during the years in which she lived in Italy – spent mainly in Rome and Naples – she worked "prodigiously". On arriving in the Eternal City, she executed the self-portrait commissioned from her by Giuseppe Pelli during her visit to Florence for the famous collection of the Gallerie degli Uffizi (inv. 1890 no. 1905) and displayed the copy made for Lord Bristol at the Académie de France à Rome, garnering plaudits and enthusiasm. In 1790, she was elected member of the Accademia di San Luca and executed a second self-portrait for this Roman institution (inv. 342). She frequented the artists working in the city, including her colleague Angelica Kauffmann, and confirmed her primacy as a high society portraitist by immortalizing the most illustrious figures of cosmopolitan Rome. They include Countess Anna Potocka (1791, private collection), Madame Victoire de France (1791, Phoenix Art Museum, inv. 1974.36) and her sister Adélaïde (La Fère, Aisne, Musée Jeanne d'Aboville, inv. MJA 124). The painter also visited palaces, museums, churches and ancient ruins and began to draw and paint landscapes and studies of the sky, mainly in pastel. Her commercial and social success, bolstered by her acknowledged talents as an artist, allowed her to rapidly rebuild the "fortune" squandered by her husband. She left Rome in April 1792, persuaded to return home. Along the way she spent time in various cities. In Parma, where she spent a few days, she was appointed member of the city's academy, to which she gave the *Portrait of the Daughter* (Parma, Galleria Nazionale, inv. 347). During her stay in Turin, she received news of the insurrection of 10 August and the attack on the Tuileries, and abandoned the idea of returning to Paris. Vigée Le Brun made her final Italian stopover in Milan, before departing for Vienna in the spring of 1792.

BIBLIOGRAPHY: Fernando Mazzocca, *Viaggio in Italia di una donna artista: i* Souvenirs *di Elisabeth Vigée le Brun 1789-1792.* Milan: Electa, 2004; *Vigée Le Brun,* exhib. cat. (New York–Ottawa 2015–2016), ed. by Joseph Baillio, Katharine Baetjer, Paul Lang. New Haven-London: Yale University Press, 2016.

Jessica Calipari

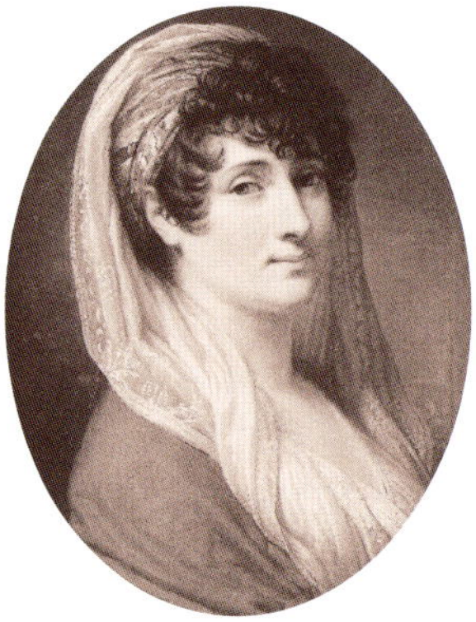

Mariana Waldstein (of Santa-Cruz)

(Vienna, 1763 – Fano, 1808)

An amateur miniaturist of Viennese origin, Mariana Fernanda Waldstein-Lichtenstein began her artistic career in Madrid after moving there in 1781 following her marriage to José Joaquín de Silva y Bazán, ninth marquis of Santa-Cruz.

According to her principal biographer, Fernández de Navarrete, in the Spanish city Mariana had the opportunity to cultivate a talent that had already become manifest earlier. She experimented with different techniques under the guidance of Isidro Carnicero before subsequently specializing in small format painting, displaying at the Real Academia de San Fernando, an institution to which she was admitted about a year after her arrival at the Spanish court. 1801 marked the start of a period of travel for the marquise, who alternated stays in Paris with returns to Spain and periods spent in Rome, Milan and Florence. In the latter city she executed a self-portrait following her admission to the academy in 1802 (inv. 2109–1890). In the Eternal City, presumably her first port of call in Italy, she frequented prominent members of Roman cosmopolitan society and the art world, such as Gaspare Landi, Pietro Benvenuti and Anton von Maron, who proposed her as a member of the Accademia di San Luca to which she was admitted in September 1803. This appointment explains the portrait of the marquise executed by Andrea Appiani in 1804 (inv. 391) and the miniature copy of Raphael's double portrait, executed in Paris and given to the institution as a reception piece in 1806 (inv. 686), the year of her final visit to Rome. On the same occasion she made various miniature copies of famous masterpieces such as Titian's *Sacred and Profane Love*, much admired by Vincenzo Camuccini, Gaspare Landi and Antonio Canova. From the sculptor, whose portrait she also painted, she commissioned the magnificent funerary monument for her deceased daughter, the Countess de Haro. In 1808 she decided to leave the Eternal City to return to her native Vienna. She died of dropsy during the journey, at Fano, aged forty-six.

BIBLIOGRAPHY: J. Soubeyroux, "Les espagnoles à l'Académie des Beaux Arts de San Fernando dans la seconde moitié du XVIIIe siècle." In *Regards sur les Espagnoles créatrices (XVIIIe-XXe siècles),* ed. by Françoise Étienvre. Paris: Presses Sorbonne Nouvelle, 2006, 75–89; David García Cueto, "Retratos y retratistas de Mariana Waldstein, IX marquesa consorte de Santa Cruz." *Goya. Revista de Arte,* no. 355 (2016), 90, 140–59.

Jessica Calipari

Andrea Appiani, ***Portrait of Marianna Waldstein (of Santa-Cruz)***, 1804. Rome, Accademia Nazionale di San Luca.

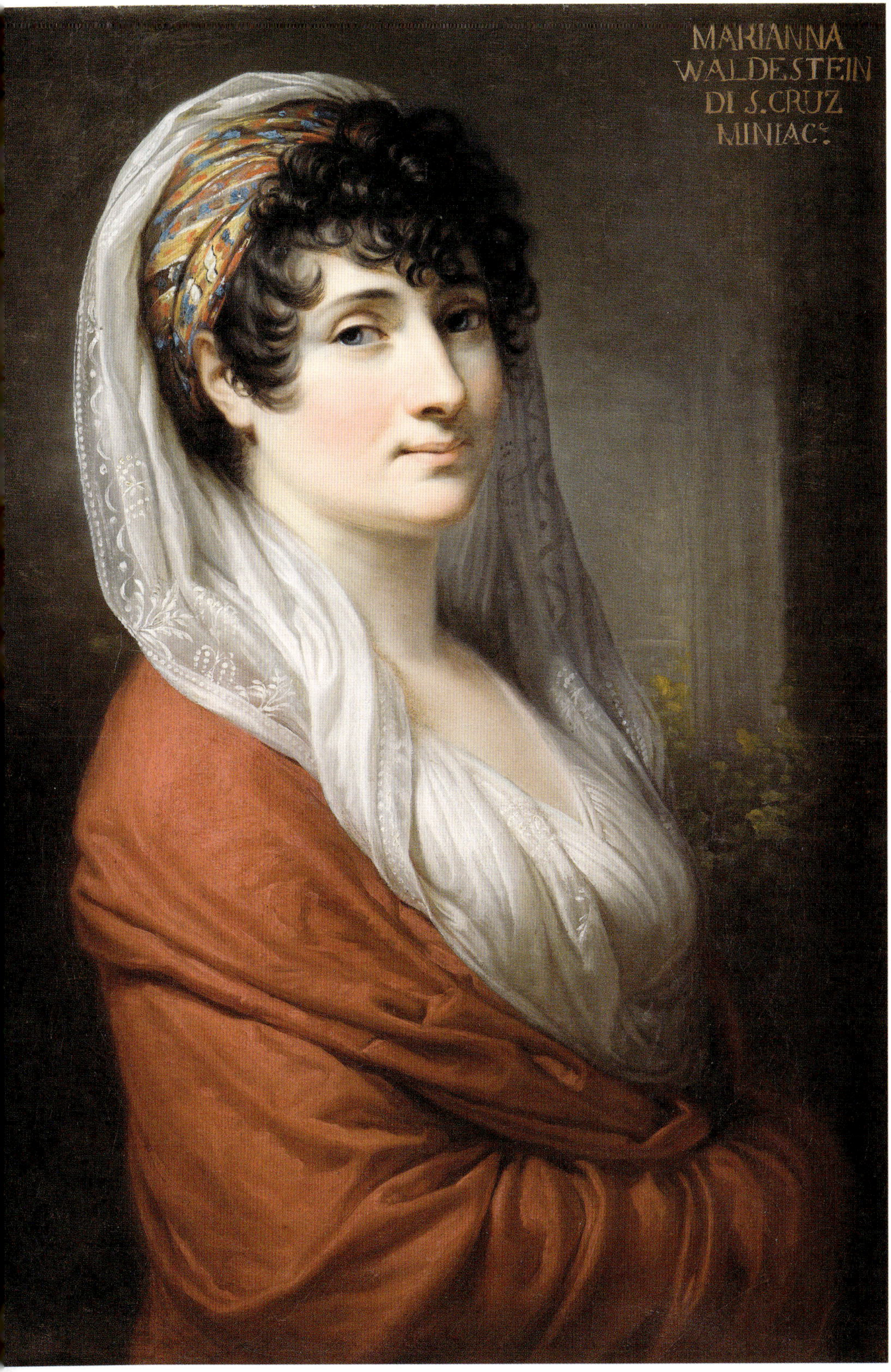
MARIANNA
WALDESTEIN
DI S.CRUZ
MINIAC.

Photo Credits

Copenaghen, Thorvaldsens Museum: 2
Ferrara, Fondazione Cavallini-Sgarbi: 55; / Le Immagini: 39
Florence, Gallerie degli Uffizi, ©Gabinetto Fotografico delle Gallerie degli Uffizi (courtesy Ministero della Cultura): 46
London, ©National Portrait Gallery 78
London, Stair Sainty Gallery: 63
Milan, Accademia di Belle Arti di Brera / Ph. Roberto Rosso: 70
Rome, ©Accademia Nazionale di San Luca: 10, 30, 47, 54, 87
Rome, Alessandra Masu Collection / Ph. Andrea Cardinali, Frascati: 75
Rome, Dario Del Bufalo Collection
Rome, Fondazione Camillo Caetani: 62
Rome, Galleria Nazionale d'Arte Moderna e Contemporanea (courtesy Ministero della Cultura): 31
Rome, Museo di Roma, Archivio iconografico / Ph. Alfredo Valeriani: cover, 18–9, 51
Rome, Pinacoteca Capitolina (Roma Capitale, Sovrintendenza Capitolina ai Beni Culturali) / Ph. Alessandra Ciniglio 82–3
©Roma Capitale, Sovrintendenza Capitolina ai Beni Culturali – Museo Napoleonico: 15, 22–3, 27, 31
Turin, Musei Reali, Galleria Sabauda / Palazzo Reale (courtesy Ministero della Cultura): 35, 58

Cover image: Virginia Barlocci (Riccardi; Mariani), *Beatrice*, *c.* 1880. Rome, Museo di Roma.

Officina Libraria
via dei Villini 10
00161 Rome

Art direction and layout
Paola Gallerani

Editorial coordinator
Giovanni Truglia

Translation
Erika Milburn

Colour separation
Giorgio Canesin

Printed by
Petruzzi stampa, Città di Castello (PG)

FSC www.fsc.org MISTO Carta | A sostegno della gestione forestale responsabile FSC® C017635

ISBN: 978-88-3367-317-2

www.officinalibraria.net
Printed in Italy

officinalibraria.net Officina.Libraria officinalibraria